George Melville Baker

Irish dialect recitations

comprising a series of the most popular selections in prose and verse

George Melville Baker

Irish dialect recitations
comprising a series of the most popular selections in prose and verse

ISBN/EAN: 9783744737845

Printed in Europe, USA, Canada, Australia, Japan

Cover: Foto ©Thomas Meinert / pixelio.de

More available books at **www.hansebooks.com**

BOSTON

LEE AND SHEPARD PUBLISHERS

NEW YORK CHARLES T. DILLINGHAM

Baker's Dialect Series

IRISH DIALECT RECITATIONS

COMPRISING A SERIES OF

THE MOST POPULAR SELECTIONS

In Prose and Verse

EDITED BY

GEORGE M. BAKER

COMPILER OF "THE READING CLUB AND HANDY SPEAKER," "THE
PREMIUM SPEAKER," "THE POPULAR SPEAKER," "THE
PRIZE SPEAKER," "THE HANDY SPEAKER," ETC.

BOSTON
LEE AND SHEPARD PUBLISHERS
NEW YORK
CHARLES T. DILLINGHAM
1888

RAND AVERY COMPANY,
ELECTROTYPERS AND PRINTERS,
BOSTON.

CONTENTS.

		PAGE
How Teddy Saved His Bacon		5
Mr. O'Hoolahan's Mistake		7
The Last of the Sarpints		9
The Irish Boy and the Priest		11
An Irish Wake		12
Biddy's Philosophy	*R. H. Stoddard*	14
Reflections on the Needle	*Cormac O'Leary*	15
The Red O'Neil	*Thomas S. Collier*	16
Deaf and Dumb	*Anna F. Burnham*	20
. *.* Murphy Explains His Son's Conduct		21
Ram for Ould Oireland		22
e Gridiron	*William B. Fowle*	23
'e " O'Meara Consolidated "	*Va. City Enterprise*	26
ddy's Metamorphosis	*Moore*	28
. *ie* Widow O'Shane's Rent		29
hy Biddy and Pat Got Married		30
Don Squixet's Ghost	*Harry Bolingbroke*	31
Mr. O'Gallagher's Three Roads to Learning	*Captain Marryat*	33
Two Irish Idyls	*Alfred Perceval Graves,*	37
The Broken Pitcher		39
Paddy's Excelsior	*Harper's Magazine*	40
The Irish Philosopher		41
Mary Maloney's Philosophy	*Philadelphia Bulletin,*	42
Bridget McRae's Wedding Anniversary	*Nina Gray*	44
Paddy O'Rafther	*Samuel Lover*	45
Pat's Reason		47
O'Branigan's Drill	*W. W. Fink*	47
Pat and the Pig		48
Pat and the Oysters		50
A Penitent	*Margaret Eytinge*	51
Mike McGaffaty's Dog	*Mark Melville*	51
Jimmy Butler and the Owl		53
Tipperary		56
Pat's Dream of Heaven		58
Biddy's Troubles		61

4   *CONTENTS.*

		PAGE
Make It Four, Yer Honor		62
The Post-Boy	Mrs. C. J. Despard	64
That Fire at the Nolans'	Life	67
Ninety-Eight		70
Pat's Bondsman	Lilian A. Moulton	71
Washee, Washee	Joaquin Miller	73
Annie's Ticket		74
O'Thello	Harper's Magazine	76
Lanty Leary	Samuel Lover	77
Katie's Answer		78
Paddy's Dream		79
Lessons in Cookery	Detroit Free Press	80
The Irish Traveller		82
Teddy's Six Bulls		82
A Miracle	Charles H. Webber	84
Pat and Miss Skitty	Bessie Bently	84
At the Rising of the Moon	Leo Casey	86
The Irish Schoolmaster		87
How Dennis Took the Pledge		89
When McGue Puts the Baby to Sleep		90
The Confession	Samuel Lover	91
Father Phil's Collection	Samuel Lover	92
St. Patrick's Martyrs		100
Pat's Correspondence	W. M. Giffin	102
Little Pat and the Parson		104
Patrick O'Rouke and the Frogs	George W. Bungay	105
Widow Malone	Charles Lever	108
The Birth of St. Patrick	Samuel Lover	109
Murphy's Mystery of the Pork Barrel		110
Paddy Blake's Echo	Samuel Lover	111
A Cook of the Period		112
Larry's on the Force	Irwin Russell	113
Pat and the Frogs	R. M. T.	114
Paddy's Courting	W. A. Eaton	116
A Bit of Gossip	Josephine Pollard	118
Paddy and His Pig		120
Teddy McGuire and Paddy O'Flynn	Amanda T. Jones	121
Paudeen O'Rafferty's Say-Voyage		125
Irish Astronomy	Charles G. Halpine	128
Paddy McGrath's Introduction to Mr. Bruin		129
Larrie O'Dee	W. W. Fink	131
Irish Coquetry		132

IRISH DIALECT RECITATIONS.

HOW TERRY SAVED HIS BACON.

EARLY one fine morning, as Terence O'Fleary was hard at work in his potato-garden, he was accosted by his gossip, Mick Casey, who he perceived had his Sunday clothes on.

"Ah! Terry, man, what would you be afther doing there wid them praties, an' Phelim O'Loughlin's berrin' goin' to take place? Come along, ma bochel! sure the praties will wait."

"Och! no," sis Terry: "I must dig on this ridge for the childers' breakfast; an' thin I'm goin' to confession to Father O'Higgins, who holds a stashin beyout there at his own house."

"Bother take the stashin!" sis Mick: "Sure that 'ud wait too." But Terence was not to be persuaded.

Away went Mick to the berrin'; and Terence, having finished "wid the praties," as he said, went down to Father O'Higgins, where he was shown into the kitchen to wait his turn for confession. He had not been long standing there before the kitchen-fire, when his attention was attracted by a nice piece of bacon which hung in the chimney-corner. Terry looked at it again and again, and wished the childer "had it home wid the praties."

"Murther alive!" says he, "will I take it? Sure the priest can spare it; an' it would be a rare thrate to Judy an' the gossoons at home, to say nothin' iv myself, who hasn't tasted the likes this many's the day." Terry looked at it again, and then turned away, saying, "I won't take it: why would I, an' it not mine, but the priest's? an' I'd have the sin iv it, sure! I won't take it," replied he;

"an' it's nothin' but the Ould Boy himself that's timptin' me. But sure it's no harm to feel it, any way." said he, taking it into his hand, and looking earnestly at it. "Och! it's a beauty; and why wouldn't I carry it home to Judy and the childer? An' sure it won't be a sin afther I confesses it."

Well, into his great-coat pocket he thrust it; and he had scarcely done so, when the maid came in and told him that it was his turn for confession.

"Murther alive! I'm kilt and ruined. horse and foot, now, joy, Terry. What'll I do in this quandary, at all, at all? By gannies! I must thry an' make the best of it, anyhow," says he to himself; and in he went.

He knelt to the priest, told his sins, and was about to receive absolution, when all at once he seemed to recollect himself, and cried out, —

"Oh! stop, stop, Father O'Higgins, dear! for goodness' sake, stop! I have one great big sin to tell yit; only, sur, I'm frightened to tell id, in the regard of niver having done the like afore, sur, niver!"

"Come!" said Father O'Higgins, "you must tell it to me."

"Why, then, your riverince, I will tell id; but, sur, I'm ashamed like."

"Oh! never mind: tell it," said the priest.

"Why, then, your riverince, I went out one day to a gintleman's house, upon a little bit of business; an' he bein' ingaged, I was showed into the kitchen to wait. Well, sur, there I saw a beautiful bit iv bacon hanging in the chimbly-corner. I looked at id, your riverince, an' my teeth began to wather. I don't know how it was, sur. but I suppose the divil timpted me, for I put it into my pocket; but, if you plaze, sur, I'll give it to you;" and he put his hand into his pocket.

"Give it to me!" said Father O'Higgins. "No, certainly not: give it back to the owner of it."

"Why, then. your riverince, sur, I offered id to him, and he wouldn't take id."

"Oh! he wouldn't, wouldn't he?" said the priest: "then take it home, and eat it yourself, with your family."

"Thank your riverince kindly!" says Terence. "an' I'll do that same immediately; but first and foremost, I'll have the absolution, if you plaze, sur."

Terence received absolution, and went home rejoicing that he had been able to save his soul and his bacon at the same time.

MR. O'HOOLAHAN'S MISTAKE.

AN amusing scene occurred in Justice Young's court-room an evening or two since. Two sons of the "ould sod," full of "chain-lightning" and law, rushed in, and, advancing to the justice's little law-pulpit at the rear of the court-room, both began talking at once.

"One at a time, if you please," said the judge.

"Judge — yer — honor — will I sphake thin?" said one of the men.

"Silence!" roared his companion. "I am here! Let me talk! Phwat do you know about law?"

"Keep still yourself, sir," said the judge. "Let him say what he wants."

"Well, I want me naime aff the paiper. That's phwat I want," said the man.

"Off what paper?" said the judge.

"Well, aff the paiper: ye ought to know what paiper. Sure, ye married me, they say."

"To whom?" asked the judge.

"Some female, sir; and I don't want her, sir. It don't go! and I want me naime aff the paiper."

"Silence!" roared the friend, bringing his huge fist down upon the little pulpit, just under the judge's nose, with a tremendous thwack. "Silence! I am here. Phwat do you know about law? Sure, yer honor, it was Tim McCloskey's wife that he married — his widdy, I mane. You married thim, yer honor."

"And I was dhrunk at the time, sir. Yis, sir; an' I was not a free aigent; an' I don't know a thing about it, sir — devil roawst me. I want me naime aff the paiper — I repudiate, sir."

"Silence! Let me spake. Phwat do you know about law?" bringing his fist down upon the judge's desk.

"But I was dhrunk: I was not at the time a free aigent."

"Silence! I am here to spake. It does not depind on that at all. It depinds — and there is the whole pint, both in law and equity — it depinds whether was the woman a sole trader or not at the time this marriage was solemnated. That is the pint, both in law and equity!"

"But I was dhrunk at the time. Divil roawst me if I

knowed I was gittin' married. I was not a free aigent. I
want the judge to taik me naime aff the paiper. It don't go."

The judge tried to explain to the man that, drunk or sober,
he was married to the woman fast enough, and, if he wanted
a divorce, he must go to another court.

"Divil burn me!" cried the man, "if I go to another
court. Ye married me, and ye can unmarry me. Taik me
naime aff the paiper!"

"Silence!" cried the friend, bringing his fist down in close
proximity to the judge's nose. "Phwat do you know about
law? I admit, judge, that he must go to a higher court;
that is (down comes the fist) if the woman can prove (whack)
that she was at the time the marriage was solemnated
(whack) a regularly ordained sole thrader (whack). On this
pint it depinds, both in law and equity."

"I have had enough of this!" cried the judge: "I cannot divorce you. You are married, and married you must
remain, for all I can do."

"Ye won't taik me naime aff the paiper, thin!"

"It would not mend the matter," said the judge.

"Ye won't taik it aff?"

"No: I won't!" fairly yelled the judge.

"Silence!" cried the partner, bringing down his fist, and
raising a cloud of dust under the judge's nose. "It depinds
whether, at the time, the woman was a regular sole"—

"Get out of here," cried the judge. "I've had about enough
of this!" at the same time rising.

"Ye won't taik it aff? Very well, thin, I'll go hoam and
devorce myself. Divil roawst me, I'll fire the thatch! I
will"—

Here he glanced toward the front door: his under jaw
drooped, he ceased speaking, and in a half-stooping posture
he went out of the back door of the office like a shot.

The valiant friend and legal adviser also glanced toward
the door, when he, too, doubled up and scooted in the footsteps of his illustrious principal.

A look at the door showed it darkened by a woman about
six feet in height, and so broad as to fill it almost from side
to side.

The judge took a look at this mountain of flesh, doubled
up, and was about to take the back track, but thought better
of it, and took refuge behind his little law-pulpit.

The mountain advanced, gave utterance in a sort of internal rumble, and then, amid fire, smoke, and burning lava, belched out, —

"Did I, or did I not, see Michael O'Hoolahan sneak out of your back door?"

"I believe O'Hoolahan is the name of one of the gentlemen who just went out," said the judge.

Advancing upon the pulpit — behind which the judge settled lower and lower — the mountain belched, —

"You be-e-lave! You know it was Michael O'Hoolahan! Now, what is all this connivin' in here about? Am I a widdy again? Did ye taik his naime aff the paiper? Did you taik it aff?"

"N-no," said the judge.

"Ye didn't? Don't ye decave me!"

"No: I give you my word of honor I didn't, couldn't — I had no right."

"It's well for ye ye didn't. I'll tache him to be rinnin' about connivin' to lave me a lone widdy agin', whin I'm makin' a jintleman of him!"

With this she sailed back to the door, where she turned, and, shaking her fist, thus adressed the tip of the judge's nose, which alone was visible above the little pulpit, —

"Now, do you mind that you lave his name on the paiper! I want no meddlin' wid a man waust I git him. No more connivin'!"

THE LAST OF THE SARPINTS.

"THE serpent, is it?" said Picket, in reply. "Sure, everybody has heard tell of the blessed St. Patrick, and how he *druve the sarpints*, and all manner of venomous things, out of Ireland — how he bothered all the *varmint* entirely; but for all that, there was one ould sarpint left, who was too cunning to be talked out of the country and made to drown himself. St. Patrick didn't well know how to manage this fellow, who was doing great havoc; till at last he bethought himself, and got a strong iron chest made, with nine boults upon it.

"So one fine morning he takes a walk to where the sarpint used to keep; and the sarpint, who didn't like the Saint in the least, — and small blame to him for that, — began to hiss and show his teeth at him like anything. 'Oh,' says St. Patrick, says he, 'where's the use of making such a piece of work about a gentleman, like myself, coming to see you? — 'tis a nice house I have got made for you agin the winter; for I'm going to civilize the whole country, man and beast,' says he, 'and you can come and look at it whenever you please, and 'tis myself will be glad to see you.'

"The sarpint, hearing such smooth words, thought that though St. Patrick had druve all the rest of the sarpints into the sea, he meant no harm to himself; so the sarpint walks fair and easy up to see him and the house he was speaking about. But when the sarpint saw the nine great boults upon the chest, he thought he was *sould*, and was for making off with himself as fast as he could.

"'Tis a nice warm house, you see,' says St. Patrick, 'and 'tis a good friend I am to you.'

"'I thank you, kindly, St. Patrick, for your civility,' says the sarpint, 'but I think it's too small it is for me;' meaning it for an excuse; and away he was going.

"'Too small!' says St. Patrick; 'stop, if you please,' says he; 'you're out in that, my boy, anyhow — I am sure 'twill fit you completely; and, I'll tell you what,' says he, 'I'll bet you a gallon of porter,' says he, 'that if you'll only try and get in, there'll be plenty of room for you.'

"The sarpint was as thirsty as he could be with his walk, and 'twas great joy to him the thoughts of doing St. Patrick out of the gallon of porter; so, swelling himself up as big as he could, he got into the chest, all but a little bit of his tail. 'There, now,' says he, 'I've won the gallon, for you see the house is too small for me, for I can't get in my tail.' When, what does St. Patrick do but he comes behind the great heavy lid of the chest, and, putting his two hands to it, down he flaps it with a bang like thunder. When the rogue of a sarpint saw the lid coming down, in went his tail like a shot, for fear of being whipped off him, and St. Patrick began at once to boult the nine iron boults.

"'Oh, murder! Won't you let me out, St. Patrick?' says the sarpint — 'I've lost the bet fairly, and I'll pay you the gallon like a man.'

"'Let you out, my darling?' says St. Patrick; 'to be sure I will, by all manner of means; but you see I haven't time now, so you must wait till to-morrow.'

"And so he took the iron chest, with the sarpint in it, and pitches it into the lake here, where it is to this hour, for certain; and 'tis the sarpint struggling down at the bottom that makes the waves upon it. Many is the living man," continued Picket, "besides myself, has heard the sarpint crying out from within the chest under the water, 'Is it to-morrow yet? — is it to-morrow yet?' which, to be sure, it never can be. And that's the way St. Patrick settled the last of the sarpints, sir."

THE IRISH BOY AND THE PRIEST.

A PRETTY Irish boy, whose parents went
By different roads to word and sacrament —
To mother's church an inclination had,
But father unto mass would *force* the lad.
Yet still the boy to church on Sunday stole,
And evidenced a wish to save his soul.
The rector eyed the youth, his zeal approved,
And gave a Bible, which he dearly loved.
This made the enraged father storm and curse,
Lock up *the book*, and use his son the worse.

At length, one Sunday morn, it came to pass,
The father dragged the struggling boy to mass;
The zealous Papists helped to *force* him in,
And begged the priest to pardon all his sin.
" No, by the mass," he said, " I cannot bless
Nor pardon — till the culprit first confess."
" Well," said the boy, " supposing I were willing,
What is your charge? " — " *I'll charge you but a shilling.*"
" Must *all men* pay, and all men make confession? "
" Yes, every man of *Catholic* profession."

" And to whom do *you* confess? " — " Why, the *dean.*"
" And does he charge you? " — " Yes, a white thirteen."
" And do your *deans* confess? " — " Yes, boy, they do
Confess to bishops, and pay sharply too! "
" Do *bishops*, sir, confess, pay, and to whom? "
" Why, they confess, and pay the CHURCH OF ROME."
" Well," quoth the boy, " all this is mighty odd! —
But does the *Pope* confess? " — " Oh, yes — to God."
" And does God charge the Pope? "—" No," quoth the priest,
" He charges nothing." — " Oh, then God's the best —
God's able to forgive, and always willing ;
To him I shall confess, and save my shilling ! "

AN IRISH WAKE.

TIM SCANLIAN, while he lived, was only a laboring-man; but he was well liked in the country, and it was expected that his funeral would be an unusually large gathering. Crowds flocked to the wake; and a great provision of tea, whiskey, pipes, and tobacco, had been made. The widow occupied her post of honor at the head of the coffin, and displayed a fair show of grief, joining in with vociferous weeping whenever the "keening" was led by the older women. She was young enough to have been the dead man's daughter, having come to his house a "slip" of a servant-girl, whom he had married, and ruled over very masterfully.

As the night wore on, the whiskey began to tell on those outside the room where the corpse lay. The noise increased, and soon apparently became loud enough to "wake the dead," as the saying is; for, to the consternation and amazement of every one present, the defunct, after a deep sigh and sundry groans, opened his eyes, and struggled up into a sitting posture! When the startled company had recovered from the shock, poor Tim was lifted out of the coffin; whiskey was liberally poured down his throat; and well wrapped up in blankets, and seated in the big chair by the fire, he gradually revived from the trance or stupor that had been mistaken for death. The last of the guests had departed from the cabin; and Tim, still propped up before the fire, was left to the care of his wife. Instead of coming near him, however, she slunk off, cringing timidly away into a dark corner behind his chair, whence she directed frightened glances at her resuscitated spouse.

"Mary!" said the man in a stern voice.

No answer.

"Are you there?" peering round, his face quivering with anger and weakness.

"Yes, Tim, I'm here," faltered Mary, without stirring.

"Bring me my stick!"

"Ah, no, Tim!—no! Sure you never rose yer hand to me yet! And 'tisn't now, when you're all as one as come back from the dead, that"—

"Bring me my stick!"

The stick was brought, and down on her knees beside the big chair flopped the cowering wife.

"Well you know what you desarve! Well you know, you young thief o' the world, that, if I was to take and beat you this blessed minute as black as a mourning-coach, 'twould be only sarving you right, after the mean, dirty, shameful turn you've done me!"

"It would, it would!" sobbed the girl.

"Look here!" gasped Tim, opening his breast, and show ing an old tattered shirt. "Look at thim rags! Look at what you dressed up me poor corpse in, shaming me before all the dacent neighbors at the wake! an' you knowing as well as I did about the elegant brand-new shirt I'd bought o' purpose for my berrin; a shirt I wouldn't have put on my living back, — no, not if I had gone naked in my skin! You knew I had it there in my chest laid up; and you grudged it to my unfortunate carcass, when I couldn't spake up for myself!"

"O Tim, darlin', forgive me!" cried Mary. "Forgive me this once, and on my two knees I promise never, never to do the likes again! I don't know what came over me at all. Sure I think the divil — Lord save us! — must have been at my elbow when I went to get out the shirt, tempt ing me, and whispering that it was a pity and a sin to put good linen like that into clay. Oh! how could I do it at all?"

"Now hearken to me, Mary;" and Tim raised the stick, and laid it on her shoulder. She knew he wouldn't beat her, even if he could with his trembling hands; but she pretended to wince and cower away. "Mind what I say: as sure as you do me the like turn again, and go for to dress me in those undacent rags, I tell you what I'll do, — I'll *walk!*"

"Oh, don't, Tim, don't!" shrieked Mary, as pale as ashes. "Murther me now, if it's plazing to you, or do any thing to me you like; but, for the love of the blessed Vargin and all the saints, keep in yer grave! I'll put the new shirt on you: my two hands'll starch it, and make it up as white as snow, after lying by so long in the old chest. Yer corpse will look lovely, niver fear! — and I'll give you the grandest wake that iver man had, even if I have to sell the pig, and part with every stick in the cabin, to buy the tay and the whiskey. I swear to you I will, darlin'. There's my hand on it this blessed night!"

"Well, mind you do, or 'twill be worse for you. And

now give me a drop of wather to drink, and put a taste of sperrits through it; for I'm like to faint with thirst and weakness."

Mary kept her promise; for such a wake was never re‑membered as Tim Scanlian's, when, soon after, the poor man really did depart this life; and the "get-up" of the "ele‑gant brand-new shirt" in which the corpse was arrayed was the admiration of all beholders.

BIDDY'S PHILOSOPHY.

WHAT would I do if you was dead?
　And when do you think of dying?
I'd stand by your bed, and hold your head,
　And cry, or pretind to be crying!
There's many a worser man nor you —
　If one knew where to find him —
And mebbe many a better, too,
　With money to leave behind him!
But you, if I was dying to-day,
　(I saw you now when you kissed her!)
I tell you, Pat, what you'd be at —
　You'd marry your widdy's sister!

You'd make an illigant corpse, indade,
　Sleeping so sound and stiddy;
If you could see yourself as you laid,
　You'd want to come back to Biddy!
You would be dressed in your Sunday bes`,
　As tidy as I could make you,
With a sprig of something on your breast,
　And the boys would come to wake you.
But you, if I was dead in your stead,
　(Do you think I never missed her?)
I tell you, Pat, what you'd be at —
　You'd marry your widdy's sister!

The undertaker would drive the hearse
　That has the big black feather;
If there was no money left in your purse,
　Your friends would club together.

They'd look at your cold remains before
    They followed you down to the ferry,
And the coaches standing at the door
    Would go to the cemetery.
But you, if I was once in the box,
    (I wonder her lips don't blister!)
I tell you, Pat, what you'd be at —
    You'd marry your widdy's sister!

When you was under the sod I'd sigh,
    And — if I could do without you —
Mebbe I've a strapping lad in my eye
    Would come here and talk about you.
A little courtin' would be divertin',
    A kind voice whispering "*Biddy!*"
And a kiss on the sly — for what's the hurt in
    A man consoling a widdy?
But you, before I was dead at all,
    (Now don't deny that you kissed her!)
I tell you, Pat, what you'd be at —
    You'd marry your widdy's sister!
                      R. H. Stoddard.

REFLECTIONS ON THE NEEDLE.

So that's Cleopathera's Needle, bedad,
    An' a square lookin' needle it is, I'll be bound;
What a powerful muscle the queen must have had
    That could grasp such a weapon an' wind it around!

Imagine her sittin' there stitchin' like mad
    Wid a needle like that in her hand! I declare
It's as big as the Round Tower of Slane, an', bedad,
    It would pass for a round tower, only it's square!

The taste of her, ordherin' a needle of granite!
    Begorra, the sight of it sthrikes me quite dumb!
An' look at the quare sort of figures upon it;
    I wondher can these be the tracks of her thumb?

I once was astonished to hear of the faste
    Cleopathera made upon pearls; but now
I declare, I would not be surprised in the laste
    If ye told me the woman had swallowed a cow!

It's aisy to see why bould Cæsar should quail
　In her presence an' meekly submit to her rule;
Wid a weapon like that in her fist I'll go bail
　She could frighten the sowl out of big Finn MacCool!

But, Lord, what poor pigmies the women are now,
　Compared with the monsthers they must have been then!
Whin the darlin's in those days would kick up a row,
　Holy smoke, but it must have been hot for the men!

Just think how a chap that goes courtin' would start
　If his girl was to prod him with that in the shins!
I have often seen needles, but boldly assart
　That the needle in front of me there takes the pins!

O, sweet Cleopathera! I am sorry you're dead;
　An' whin laving this wontherful needle behind
Had ye thought of bequathin' a spool of your thread
　An' yer thimble an' scissors, it would have been kind.

But pace to your ashes, ye plague of great men,
　Yer strenth is departed, yer glory is past;
Ye'll never wield sceptre or needle again,
　An' a poor little asp did yer bizzness at last!

CORMAC O'LEARY.

THE RED O'NEIL.

HIGH over Galway's stormy tide, in years that long have
　flown,
A grim and gloomy castle raised its mass of sombre stone:
The sullen flood that by it rolled was not more dark and
　drear,
And when its great, black portals swung, the land was full
　of fear.

Its chieftain was the Red O'Neil, a warrior brave and bold,
But hate's fierce longing filled his heart and made it hard
　and cold;
And when his plume and banner flew along the restless
　seas,
'　The bitter wailing of his foes rose through the rising breeze.

His keen sword never proved untrue, his lance was sharp
    and sure;
His stout ship braved the roughest blast, his horse the
    wildest moor;
The Saxon maidens shrank in dread when echoed through
    the hall
His wrathful name, and warriors sprang where swords
    hung on the wall.

Not long had Red O'Neil's bright sword been bitter to the
    foe —
Not long his fiery soul had grown unheeding of their woe —
But now the sanguine flame that glowed along his foray's
    path,
Shone with the lurid light that told a never-dying wrath.

Bright as the golden light that gleams among the morning
    mist,
Was Lady Nora's yellow hair, when by the sunlight kissed;
The lustrous glory of her eyes, blue as a clear June sky,
Was rich with all the tenderness that gives love sweet
    reply.

The dainty color of her lips, the fairness of her face,
The clinging of her little hand, her womanhood's pure
    grace,
The music of her ringing voice, the gladness of her mien,
Had made the Red O'Neil bow low, and claim her as his
    queen.

Beyond the stern and barren lands along the foaming sea,
Whose tempest-waves swept fiercely up from many a wide
    degree,
Through plains all rich with bending wheat the rapid river
    flowed,
And by the forest's dusky aisles its sunlit water glowed.

The far hills looming to the sky shone in the opal haze,
And robins sang their merry songs in all the orchard ways;
The harvesters were in the field, and herds with tinkling
    bells,
Stood knee-deep in the fragrant grass that clothed the
    southward dells.

Then proud with floating banners, and lances keen and
strong,
A brave array of steel-clad knights up from the eastward
throng;
King Henry's Saxon warriors sweep on with ruthless
speed,
And death and ruin show the track of every snorting steed.

The Lady Nora's couchant hound, growls as he hears the
clash
Of crossing swords, and spears that swift through shining
bucklers crash;
Then springs to meet the knight, whose foot falls heavy on
the stair,
While his fair mistress stands at bay, draped in dishevelled
hair.

Woe! to the cruel hand that dealt such hard and dastard
blow;
For down the broad stone steps, the streams of red blood
slowly flow;
And close beside her faithful hound the Lady Nora lies;
Death's chill has stilled his loyal heart; death's cold has
dimmed her eyes.

They brought the tidings to O'Neil.   Out sprang his gleam-
ing blade,
And quick a thousand stalwart men for battle stood arrayed;
Then swift along the river bank the clattering horses sped,
Their guides the ruined cottages, and peasants stark and
dead.

For years, upon a lonely moor, heaped round with mossy
stones,
Was seen a ghastly gathering of white and crumbling
bones.
It marked the place where Red O'Neil rushed on De Courcy's
spears,
And gave the Saxon maids and wives a heritage of tears.

The level lances grimly shone, and plumes were flying
wide,
And then O'Neil's wild warriors charged, a shouting, surg-
ing tide;

And back and forth the mad ranks swayed, till in the hot-
    test fray,
O'Neil and his black charger barred De Courcy's onward
    way.

The serried lines fell back, and left a narrow circle clear,
And firm each chieftain's strong hand grasped his battle-
    crimsoned spear;
Then spurring on their fiery steeds, they charge each other
    home,
And stout De Courcy's shattered mail grows red with
    bloody foam.

Then fled his knights, and carnage reigned. The dead lay
    white and still
Along the moor, and in the wood, and on the wind-swept
    hill.
Not one was left to tell how fierce and fell had been the
    fight,
But blazing castles told the tale amid the gloom of night.

The Lady Nora slept in peace, but vengeance in her name
Shone on the sea, and lit the land with many a baleful
    flame;
The terror of the Saxon lords, the chief with keenest steel,
And hand as tireless as his hate, was her liege-knight,
    O'Neil.

King Henry's warriors could not curb his red, destructive
    course,
And for long years his castle's wall braved all their mail-
    clad force;
He fought them till his hair was white, and weak and slow
    his breath,
And free, and dreaded by his foes, sank slowly into death.

Oh! would that Erin's cause now had ten thousand souls as
    strong,
Swayed, not by hate, but high resolve and scorn of kingly
    wrong;
Then would the beacon fires of hope light up the purple
    sky,
And from the hills, the Emerald flag of Erin's freedom fly!
                THOS. S. COLLIER.

DEAF AND DUMB.

Oh, a wild little slip was young Kitty McRea!
　So saucy and daring, so dimpled and sweet;
A foot of the lightest, a hand of the whitest,
　She brought the whole village to sue at her feet.

Gay Kitty was guarded and kept like a nun :
　She'd greet you demurely, the whole world might see.
She wore a prim shaker, and dressed like a Quaker,
　And 'neath all disguises was — Kitty McRea!

There came to the town a professor of ink,
　A dashing young penman : he published his plan ;
Declared himself willing to give for a shilling
　A lesson to any child, woman, or man.

To their sense of compassion he wisely appealed :
　He was deaf, he was dumb, — would they give him their
　　mite ?
Papas read with pleasure, and cried, " What a treasure !
　There'll be no love-making while learning to write."

The maidens flocked eagerly into the hall :
　The teacher began his instructions with glee;
Though some had a notion he showed more devotion
　To *Kitty* than might have pleased father McRea.

The handsome young teacher was freely discussed :
　" Such lovely, sad eyes ! "   The girls voted it " mean."
" Such a pity ! I'd just like to kiss him ! " said Kitty.
　" *You may !* " he said softly.   Imagine the scene !

Kitty fainted ; then fled, with her cheeks all aflame.
　They met in the garden that night after tea :
Well pleased with his hoaxing, the lad turned to coaxing, —
　" Pray do not be angry, dear Kitty McRea ! "

Who now was so bashful as Kitty McRea,
　The saucy and daring, the dimpled and sweet?
Without further parley, behold the finale, —
　Gay Kitty soon wedded this deaf and-dumb cheat.
　　　　　　　　　　　　　ANNA F. BURNHAM.

MR. MURPHY EXPLAINS HIS SON'S CONDUCT.

THAT boy, do ye mind, isn't yet seventeen,
Ye'd imagine in tricks of the world he was green;
He'd always such gintle and innocent ways
He made me belave him as good as you plaze,
An' now I find out that for three months at laste,
That boy's been indulgin' his love-making taste,
It's Nora McCarty, the daughter of Tim,
Who seems to possess an attraction for him.
The two are about of the same age and size.
She's a dacent young thing, wid a pair of black eyes
That twinkle and seem to be laughin' when sure
The rest of her face looks extremely demure.
Though she's elegant teeth to be shown by a smile,
An' her black hair is banged in American style,
An' in truth, altogether, she looks mighty fine,
For to be makin' love wid that Johnny of mine.
Sure I'd never have found out the sacret from him,
But I learned it by going to call upon Tim;
The night it was dark — 'twas a little past eight —
An', as quietly walking I came to the gate,
I heard whispered talkin', an' afther, a sound
Like a fut comin' out o' the mud. I looked round,
An' beheld the young lovers in hivenly bliss.
He'd his arm round her waist an' was takin' a kiss.
Well, I sazed the young rogue be the ear, and sez I:
"Now what are yez doin'?" He tried to reply.
I hollered: "Hi! not a dang word from yer head:
Ye jist thravel home an' go right to yer bed.
An' for you, miss — " I said — I was thrying to look
An' spake very sternly, by way of rebuke —
"You know that your father an' mother'd be wild
If they were to learn of this thrick of their child."
An' thin Nora spoke an' I thought I could hear
A sound in her voice that was much like a tear;
"Oh, plaze, Mr. Murphy, forgive us, you might,
It's my fault, not Johnny's." Bedad, she was right!
But I tried to look stern, an' I said "It is sad
That two children like you should be actin' so bad;
An' I niver must hear of such actions agin!

Now you, Johnny, go home, an' you, Nora, run in."
They ran. I should rightly have taken a shtick
An' have bate the young divil to pay for the thrick.
But indade I can't blame him for kissin' the elf,
Be me love of ould Ireland, I'd do it meself!

A RAM FOR OULD OIRELAND.

MR. PATRICK MULCAHEY made a morning call upon the
Widow O'Flaherty at her castle on the rocks in the upper
part of this city. He was attired in his best and the pre-
liminaries of politeness between the distinguished guest and
the superb *chatelaine* were all that the occasion could call for.

"I kem to ax yez," then remarked the Mulcahey, "phwat
ye're willin' to do for the cause this mornin'."

"Phwat cause is that, now, Misther Mulcahey?"

"An' phwat should it be, mim, but the cause av ould Oireland?"

"Sure, an' I'm gettin' toired, sor. Many's the dime an'
many's the dollar I've paid in till the cause; but still they do
be shootin' an' hangin' the byes, an' the bloodhy Saxin gits
fat on the best blood av ould Oireland."

"It won't be fur long now, Misthress O'Flaherty. We're
raisin' a fund to pay fur a ram."

"A ram is it? An' phwat wud yez be doin' wid a ram?"

"A ram, Misthress O'Flaherty, wud butt the shtuffin' out
av the biggest ironclad that iver floated, an' sink the British
navy quicker'n a thirsty man wud take a drink, an' shwape
the bloodhy Saxin from the says."

"It's a quare notion intoirely, sor. Is it a ram that wud
shwim in the say?"

"In the say, and over the say, an' undher the say, Misthress
O'Flaherty. An' thin, mim, it's so aisy to kape, wance we
git it. Only a coal-oil can, as I may say."

"Thrue for yez, Mr. Mulcahey. Or a tematy can, or anny
other kind av a can, wid a few yards av thayater bills for a
lunch."

"Phwat will yez give, thin, Misthress O'Flaherty?"

"If it's a ram will do the wurruk, sor, I'll take the whole
ixpinse on mesilf."

"The whole ixpinse? Do yez know phwat ye're sayin', mim?"

"Throth an' I do, sor. I'll giv the last bit av propherty I've got to the cause av ould Oireland. I'll giv yez Teddy, me own billy-goat, the pride av Shantytown; an' I pity the Saxin that wud shtand forneust him. Look at him, sor, as he climbs the rocks! By the same token, Misther Mulcahey, ye'd better shlip quietly dune the back way, as Teddy has set his two eyes on yez, and he'd butt the last board off the shanty but phwat he'd git at yez."

As Mr. Mulcahey tumbled down the cliff, the fair *chatelaine* consoled him with a promise to keep the ram until he should call for it.

------◆------

THE GRIDIRON.

THE CAPTAIN, PATRICK, AND THE FRENCHMAN.

Patrick. Well, captain, whereabouts in the wide world *are* we? Is it Roosia, Proosia, or the Jarmant Oceant?

Captain. Tut, you fool! it's France.

Patrick. Tare an' ouns! do you tell me so? and how do you know it's France, captain dear?

Captain. Because we were on the coast of the Bay of Biscay when the vessel was wrecked.

Patrick. Throth, I was thinkin' so myself. And now, captain jewel, it is I that wishes we had a gridiron.

Captain. Why, Patrick, what puts the notion of a gridiron into your head?

Patrick. Because I'm starving with hunger, captain dear.

Captain. Surely you do not intend to eat a gridiron, do you?

Patrick. Ate a gridiron! bad luck to it! no. But if we had a gridiron, we could dress a beefsteak.

Captain. Yes; but where's the beefsteak, Patrick?

Patrick. Sure, couldn't we cut it off the pork?

Captain. I never thought of that. You are a clever fellow, Patrick. (*Laughing.*)

Patrick. There's many a thrue word said in joke, captain. And now, if you will go and get the bit of pork that we saved from the wrack, I'll go to the house there beyant, and ax some of them to lind me the loan of a gridiron.

Captain. But, Patrick, this is France, and they are all foreigners here.

Patrick. Well, and how do you know but I am as good a furriner myself as any o' them?

Captain. What do you mean, Patrick?

Patrick. Parley voo frongsay?

Captain. Oh! you understand French, then, is it?

Patrick. Throth, you may say that, captain dear.

Captain. Well, Patrick, success to you. Be civil to the foreigners, and I'll be back with the pork in a minute.

[*He goes out.*

Patrick. Ay, sure enough, I'll be civil to them; for the Frinch are always mighty p'lite intirely, and I'll show them I know what good manners is. Indade, and here comes munseer himself, quite convaynient. (*As the Frenchman enters, Patrick takes off his hat, and, making a low bow, says:*) God save you, sir, and all your children. I beg your pardon for the liberty I take, but it's only being in disthress in regard of ating, that I make bowld to trouble ye; and if you could lind me the loan of a gridiron, I'd be intirely obleeged to ye.

Frenchman (*staring at him*). Comment!

Patrick. Indade, it's thrue for you. I'm tathered to paces, and God knows I look quare enough; but it's by rason of the storm that dhruv us ashore jist here, and we're all starvin'.

Frenchman. Je m'y t — (*pronounced* zhe meet).

Patrick. Oh! not at all! by no manes! we have plenty of mate ourselves, and we'll dhress it, if you'd be plased jist to lind us the loan of a gridiron, sir. (*Making a low bow.*)

Frenchman (*staring at him, but not understanding a word*).

Patrick. I beg pardon, sir; but maybe I'm undher a mistake, but I thought I was in France, sir. Ain't you all furriners here? Parley voo frongsay?

Frenchman. Oui, monsieur.

Patrick. Then, would you lind me the loan of a gridiron, if you plase? (*The Frenchman stares more than ever, as if anxious to understand.*) I know it's a liberty I take, sir, but it's only in the regard of bein' cast away; and if you plase, sir, parley voo frongsay?

Frenchman. Oui, monsieur, oui.

Patrick. Then would you lind me the loan of a gridiron, sir, and you'll obleege me?

Frenchman. Monsieur, pardon, monsieur,—

Patrick (*angrily*). By my sowl, if it was you was in disthress, and if it was to owld Ireland you came, it's not only the gridiron they'd give you, if you axed it, but something to put on it too, and a dhrop of dhrink into the bargain. Can't you understand your own language? (*Very slowly.*) Parley — voo — frongsay — munseer?

Frenchman. Oui, monsieur; oui, monsieur, mais—

Patrick. Then lind me the loan of a gridiron, I say, and bad scram to you.

Frenchman (*bowing and scraping*). Monsieur, je ne l'entend —

Patrick. Phoo! the divil sweep yourself and your *long tongs!* I don't want a tongs at all, at all. Can't you listen to rason?

Frenchman. Oui, oui, monsieur: certainement, mais —

Patrick. Then lind me the loan of a gridiron, and howld your prate. (*The Frenchman shakes his head, as if to say he did not understand: but Patrick, thinking he meant it as a refusal, says, in a passion*): Bad cess to the likes o' you! Throth, if you were in my counthry, it's not that-a-way they'd use you. The curse o' the crows on you, you owld sinner! The divil another word I'll say to you. (*The Frenchman puts his hand on his heart, and tries to express compassion in his countenance.*) Well, I'll give you one chance more, you owld thafe! Are you a Christhian, at all, at all? Are you a furriner that all the world calls so p'lite? Bad luck to you! Do you understand your mother tongue? Parley voo frongsay? (*Very loud.*) Parley voo frongsay?

Frenchman. Oui, monsieur, oui, oui.

Patrick. Then, thunder and turf! will you lind me the loan of a gridiron? (*The Frenchman shakes his head, as if he did not understand; and Pat says vehemently:*) The curse of the hungry be on you, you owld negarly villain! the back of my hand and the sowl of my fut to you! May you want a gridiron yourself yet! And wherever I go, it's high and low, rich and poor, shall hear of it, and be hanged to you!

William B. Fowle.

THE "O'MEARA CONSOLIDATED."

"THEY met by chance, the usual way," among the daughters of the wife of Adam. Said the one neighbor unto the other, —

"Good-mornin' till ye, Mrs. O'Meara."

Said the other unto the one, —

"Thank ye kindly, good-mornin', Mrs. McCracken. Yer lookin' well this mornin'."

"Och, but it's kind ways ye have, Mrs. O'Meara: ye'd be spakin' the cheerin' words if ye saw a poor body wid a fut in the grave. But I'm far from feelin' well: it's the ould distress in me chist, dear. It's airly ye're abroad the day, Mrs. O'Meara, but ye're always so industrious an' drivin'."

"Ye flatther me, Mrs. McCracken; but it's only in drivin' that there's ony thrivin' at these times — wid God's blessin', av course."

"Thrue fer ye, Mrs. O'Meara; an' thruly it's snug ye air at home now, mainin' but the honest words I shpake, an' no flatthery."

"Wid the blessin' o' God we're doin' fairly, — fairly, Mrs. McCracken."

"I wush I could get the saycret, Mrs. O'Meara. My Michael works ivery blessed day in the mines, but nothin' stays wid us."

"Do you collect assissments, Mrs. McCracken?"

"Assissments, Mrs. O'Meara? what would I be doin' wid collectin' assissments? Bad cess to it, woman: it's the other way wid us; for Michael he do be payin' assissments on this an' on that, ivery blessed month almost."

"An' where does he pay them, dear?"

"To the broker-shops, sure: where else would he pay thim, Mrs. O'Meara?"

"Why, to yourself, darlin'."

"To me, Mrs. O'Meara?"

"To yourself! Where else should he be payin' thim?"

"What for would he be payin' assissments to me?"

"What for does my Patrick pay assissments to me, but because I livil 'em on him, my dear?"

"On him? An' what is it for, darlin'?"

"It's for the stock he holds in the corporation, dear, — the interest he has in the O'Meara Consolidated. Do ye undershtand that now, — the O'M-e-ara Con-shol-idated?"

" What would that be, dear ? "

" Originally it was Patrick O'Meara and Nora McCue, but was incorporated as the O'Meara Consolidated in 1865; first issue of stock in 1865, wid a new issue ivery two years since. It's what they call a close corporation, I belave; and I am both President and Board of Directhors, hold the controlling intrust, and livil assissment."

" I don't understand it at all, Mrs. O'Meara. An' what is that ye livil assissments on, dear ? "

" On the stock, to be sure, woman, — on the live stock, do ye see? six shares now."

" Do you mane the childer? "

" What else would I mane? I'll tell ye, dear, for I see yer wits are wool-gatherin'. Ye see, for a long time Pathrick was buyin' this wild cat, an' that wild cat, an' all the cats was livilin' assissments, an' he a-payin' 'em an' kapin' us all at the point of shtarvation. I saw how things was goin', so I jist brought out on him the home incorporation; an' I says to him, ' Here now, sir, is the O'Meara Consolidated, a square location, secured by a patent, wid but six shares in it, an' showin' well as far as developed; now I livil on it my first assissment of twinty dollars a share.' Says he, ' Nora, ye're wus nor the wild cats: ye take me whole month's wages !' — ' Thrue,' says I ; ' and I'll honestly spind ivery cint in improvements for the benefit of the company.' "

" An' did he shtand the assissment, Mrs. O'Meara? "

" He did, for he thought it a good joke at first; an' for two or three months he paid like a man."

" Thin he quit payin' ? "

" He did."

" An' what thin, Mrs. O'Meara? "

" I sould him out."

" Sould him out ! How could you sell him out ? "

" Well, dear, he had due and legal notice. I first of all tould him it would be delinquent on such a day in the board ; thin that it was advertised delinquent, an' that such a time would come the day o' sale. He thought it was a good joke, but when he kem home that evenin' he had no supper. I didn't cook a warm male in a month : I sint a lot o' furniture to the auction, an' cut him off in ivery way in his home comforts."

" An' what then, dear ? "

" **He never since refused to pay his regular assissments.**"

"Och, it's a wise woman ye air, Mrs. O'Meara. Good-mornin' till ye; an' wid the help o' God I'll incorporate the McCracken Consolidated this blissed day, an' livil me first assissment before I resht me haid on me pilly the night."

Virginia City Enterprise.

PADDY'S METAMORPHOSIS.

ABOUT fifty years since, in the days of our daddies,
   That plan was commenced which the wise now applaud,
Of shipping off Ireland's most turbulent Paddies,
   As good raw materials for *settlers* abroad.
Some West India island, whose name I forget,
   Was the region then chose for this scheme so romantic;
And such the success the *first* colony met,
   That a *second* soon after set sail o'er the Atlantic.
Behold them now safe at the long looked for shore,
   Sailing between banks that the Shannon might greet,
And thinking of friends whom, but two years before,
   They had sorrowed to lose, but would soon again meet.
And hark, from the shore a glad welcome there came —
   "Arrah, Paddy from Cork, is it you, my sweet boy?"
While Pat stood astounded to hear his own name
   Thus huzzaed by blackey, who capered for joy!
Can it possibly be? Half amazement, half doubt:
   Pat listens again — rubs his eyes and looks steady;
Then heaves a deep sigh, and in horror yells out,
   "Father's blood! only think, black and curly already!"
Deceived by that well mimicked brogue in his ears,
   Pat read his own doom in those wool-headed figures,
And thought, what a climate, in less than two years
   To turn a whole cargo of Pats into *niggers.*
Tis thus, but alas, by a marvel more true
   Than is told in this rival of Ovid's best stories —
Your Whigs, when in office a short year or two,
   By a *lusus naturæ,* all turn into Tories.
And thus when I hear them "strong measures" advise,
   Ere the seats that they sit on have time to get steady,
I say, while I listen with tears in my eyes,
   "Father's blood! only think, black and curly already."

MOORE.

THE WIDOW O'SHANE'S RENT.

Whist, there! Mary Murphy, doan think me insane,
But I'm dyin' ter tell ye of Widder O'Shane;
She as lives in the attic nixt mine, doan ye know,
An' does the foine washin' fer ould Misther Schnow.

Wid niver a chick nor a child ter track in,
Her kitchen is always as nate as a pin;
An' her cap an' her apron is always that clane —
Och, a moighty foine gurrel is the Widder O'Shane.

An' wud ye belave me, on Sathurday night
We heard a rough stip comin' over our flight;
An' Mike, me ould man, he jist hollered to me,
"Look out av the door an' see who it moight be."

An' I looked, Mary Murphy, an' save me if there
Wusn't Thomas Mahone on the uppermost stair!
(He's the lan'lord. ye've seen him yerself, wid a cane),
An' he knocked on the door of the Widder O'Shane.

An' I whispered to Michael, "Now what can it mane
That his worship is calling on Widder O'Shane?"
(Rint day comes a Friday with us, doan ye see,
So I knew that it wusn't collictin' he'd be.)

"It must be she owes him some money fer rint,
Though the neighbors do say that she pays to the cint.
You take care of the baby, Michael Brady," says I,
"An' I'll pape through the keyhole, I will, if I die."

The howly saints bliss me! what shudn't I see
But the Widder O'Shane sittin' pourin' the tea!
An' the landlord wus there — Misther Thomas Ma-
    hone —
A-sittin' one side ov the table alone.

An' he looked at the Widder O'Shane, an' sez he,
"It's a privilege great that ye offer ter me;
Fer I've not sat down by a woman's side
Since I sat by her that I once called me bride.

An' is it ye're poor now, Widder O'Shane?
Ye're a dacent woman, tidy an' clane;
An' we're both av us here in the world alone —
Wud ye think of unitin' wid Thomas Mahone?"

Then the Widder O'Shane put the tea-kettle down,
An' she sez, "Misther Thomas, yer name is a crown,
I take it most gladly"— An' then me ould man
Hollered, "Bridget, cum in here quick as yer can!"

So then, Mary Murphy, I riz off that floor,
An' run into me attic, an' bolted the door;
An' I sez to me Michael, "Now, isn't it mane?
She'll have no rint to pay, will that Widder O'Shane!"

WHY BIDDY AND PAT GOT MARRIED.

" Oh, why did you marry him, Biddy?
    Why did you take Pat for your spouse ?
Sure, he's neither purty nor witty;
    And his hair is as red as a cow's.
You might had your pick, had you waited:
    You'd done a dale better with Tim;
And Phelim O'Toole was expectin';
    You couldn't do better, nor him.
You talk of us young people courtin':
    Pray tell how your courtin' began,
When you were a widdy woman,
    And he was a widdy man."

" Tim and Pat, miss, you see, was acquainted
    Before they came over the sea,
When Pat was a courtin' Norah,
    And Tim was a-courtin' me.
She did not know much, the poor Norah;
    Nor, for that matter, neither did Pat:
He had not the instinct of some one;
    But no one had then told him that.
But he soon found it out for himself, —
    For life at best's but a span, —
When I was a widdy woman,
    And he was a widdy man.

" I helped him to take care of Norah ;
And, when he compared her with me,
He saw, as he whispered one evening,
What a woman one woman could be.
She went out like the snuff of a candle:
Then the sickness seized upon Tim,
And we watched by his bedside together ;
It was such a comfort to him !
I was not alone in my weeping ;
Our tears in the same channel ran :
For I was a widdy woman,
And he was a widdy man.

" We had both had our troubles, mavourneen,
Though neither, perhaps, was to blame ;
And we both knew by this what we wanted,
And were willing to pay for the same.
We knew what it was to be married ;
And, before the long twelvemonth had flown,
We had made up our minds it was better
Not to live any longer alone.
We wasted no time shilly-shally,
Like you, miss, and Master Dan ;
For I was a widdy woman,
And he was a widdy man."

DON SQUIXET'S GHOST.

" Well, now, spakin' o' Father Doyle, reminds me of the
time whin I fust dug his peaytees for him ; let me see ; I'm
sure I don't know how many years agone, now ; but faix, 'tis
meself was only a big lump of a gurrul thin.   Oah ! but I'll
niver forget that day, if I lives to be as ould as Buckley's goat.

" Me and Biddy Morrissy were digging his rivirince's peaytees, — 'twas about tin o'clock in the morning, — and turning
up the painted ladies as purty as iver you see, whin along come
the ould rousther, and a half a dozen hens wid him, strutting
along, and pecking the peaytees like fine fellows ; and 'twas

niver a bit of use in uz sayin' 'whist!' for there the ould haythen 'ud peck and peck, scratch and scratch, till says I, 'Me
boy, I'll soon see whether or no me or you is the better man;
so I ups wid a big lump of a peaytee and laves 'im have it in
the eye; and over he goes, flipperty-flap, as dead as a herring.

"'Och, mallia!' says Biddy, says she; 'now, Kitty, you may
go and hang yerself,' says she, 'fur his riv'rince 'll niver forgive
ye killin' that bird,' says she, half-frightened out of her wits.

"'Faix, I don't care,' says I. 'What business had he peckin'
the peaytees, thin?' says I, all of a trimble.

"'Oh,' says she, 'you'll know what; and, by the same token,
here comes himself now; and you'd better dig a hole as quick
as you can, and pitch the ould rousther in it,' says she.

"So I looks round, and, sure enough, there was his riv'rince
walking slowly towards us, in the trench, wid a pinch of snuff
betune his finger and thumb, lookin' to the one side and the
other. Well, begannies, it wasn't long I was digging a hole,
and covering up the ould rousther in it, and scatterin' the peaytees over the place; and thin I felt as guilty as if it was a man
I murdered. By and by himself comes along; me heart was
thumping away inside; ye could hear it a mile off, as one may say.

"His riv'rince talked about the weather, and the peaytees, and
this and that, and there was his fut widin a yard of the place.

"'Honey,' says he, 'you shouldn't lave the hens be after pecking the peaytees!' says he; 'they'll spoil more than they're
worth,' says he.

"'Humph! 'tis meself can't keep 'em away,' says I.

"'Oh, botheration! but you must drive 'em away,' says he.

"'Faix, they won't stay druv,' I sez.

"'Why, then, Kitty,' says he, 'my honey,' says he, 'you must
knock 'em down,' says he.

"'Oh, wisha, good-morrow to ye, Father Doyle,' says I.

"'Why so?' says he.

"'Is it knock 'em down?' says I.

"'Yes,' says he, 'it is.'

"'Humph!' says I; 'if I did that same, maybe yer riv'rince 'ud
niver forgive me for doing av it!' says I.

"'Yes, I would, honey; why not?' says he.

"'What, if I killed one of yer hens?' says I.

"'Did I say kill?' says he; 'I said, knock 'em down, that's all.'

"'Hah, yer riv'rince,' says I, 'I'm thinkin' I won't thry it!'

"Oh, didn't I feel as if I wasn't spakin' the truth to him!

"'Humph!' says he, lookin' round, and takin' a pinch of

snuff; ' it surprises me not to see Don Squixet here, any way; he's always the first into mischief, and the last to lave it.'

" Dad, thinks I to meself, if he means the ould rousther, he's the fust to lave it this time, any way. • But,' says I, • and who's Don Squixet ? ' I axes, wid me heart into me mouth.

" ' Ha ! that's what I call the ould cock,' says he ; ' but the rascal is up to some mischief now, I go bail, or he'd be here,' says Father Doyle.

" Well, whether to down on me two knees (savin' yer pris- ence) and confess all, or lave him to find it out, I didn't know ; when all to once the peaytees right furnenst us begun to move, and roll the one over the other.

" ' Oah ! what's that, Kitty ? ' cries Father Doyle. ' Be the powers, there's something coming up through the yearth ! '

" Faix, 'twas meself thought I'd sink down through it ; for just then up comes the head of the ould rousther himself, bad scran to him, lookin' round to make out where he was. Awe ! I couldn't tell yees how I felt. I fell down on me knees, and axed his riv'rince to forgive a poor crayter the sin av it. But, by and by, when the ould scamp got up and shuck himself, and clapped his wings, and crowed, be dad, I thought his riv'rince would split laughing, as well as Biddy. And when Father Doyle could spake, says he, wiping his eyes wid his kurcher, ' Kitty,' says he, ' always be sure a body's dead,' says he, ' be- fore you inters it,' he says. ' But see now, if you kill any av 'em outright, another time,' says he, ' just bring the remains to me,' he says, ' and we'll have a dish of broth out of it, anyway,' says he. And wid that, he set up a-laughin' again, and walked off, shakin' his sides ; and I s'pose, if he told that story once, he did the Lord knows how many times. But he niver seed me, to this day, but he allus axed when I seen Don Squixet's Ghost last."　　HARRY BOLINGBROKE.

MR. O'GALLAGHER'S THREE ROADS TO LEARNING.

ADAPTED FROM "PERCIVAL KEENE."

MR. O'GALLAGHER sat upon his throne. I say "throne," because he had not a desk, as schoolmasters generally have, but a sort of square dais about eighteen inches high, on which was placed another oblong superstructure of the same height, serving him for a seat: both parts were covered with some patched and torn old drugget; and upon subsequent examination I found them to consist of three old claret-cases without covers, which he had probably picked up very cheap, two of them turned upside down so as to form the lower square, and the third placed in the same way, upside down, upon the two lower. Mr. O'Gallagher sat in great dignity upon the upper one, with his feet on the lower, being thus sufficiently raised upon an eminence to command a view of the whole of his pupils in every part of the school. He was not a tall man, but very square-built, with carroty hair and very bushy red whiskers: to me he appeared a most formidable person, especially when he opened his large mouth and displayed his teeth, when I was reminded of the sign of the Red Lion, close to my mother's house. I certainly never had been before so much awed during my short existence, as I was with the appearance of my pedagogue, who sat before me somewhat in the fashion of a Roman tribune, holding in his hand a short round ruler, as if it were his truncheon of authority. I had not been a minute in the school before I observed him to raise his arm; away went the ruler, whizzing through the air, until it hit the skull of the lad for whom it was intended, at the other end of the schoolroom. The boy, who had been talking to his neighbor, rubbed his poll, and whined.

"Why don't you bring back my ruler, you spalpeen?" said Mr. O'Gallagher. "Be quick, Johnny Target, or it will end in a blow-up."

The boy, who was not a little confused with the blow, sufficiently recovered his senses to obey the order, and, whimpering as he came up, returned the ruler to the hands of Mr. O'Gallagher.

"That tongue of yours will get you into more trouble than it will business, I expect, Johnny Target: it's an unruly member, and requires a constant ruler over it." Johnny Target rubbed his head, and said nothing.

"Master Keene," said he after a short pause, "did you see what a tundering tump on the head that boy got just now? and do you know what it was for?"

"No," replied I.

"Where's your manners, you animal? 'No!' If you plase, for the future, you must not forget to say 'No, sir,' or 'No, Mr. O'Gallagher.' D'ye mind me! Now say 'Yes' — what?"

"Yes; what."

"Yes, what! you little ignoramus! say 'Yes, Mr. O'Gallagher,' and recollect, as the parish clerk says, 'this is the last time of asking.'"

"Yes, Mr. O'Gallagher."

"Ah! now, you see, there's nothing like coming to school; you've learnt manners already : and now, to go back again, as to why Johnny Target had the rap on the head, which brought tears into his eyes. I'll just tell you, it was for talking. You see, the first thing for a boy to learn is, to hold his tongue : and that shall be your lesson for the day; you'll just sit down there ; and if you say one word during the whole time you are in the school, it will end in a blowup : that means on the present occasion, that I'll skin you alive as they do the eels, which, being rather keen work, will just suit your constitution."

"Now, Mr. Keene," said he, "you'll be so good as to lend me your ears, that is, to listen while I talk to you a little bit. D'ye know how many roads there are to larning? Hold your tongue : I ask you because I know you don't know, and because I'm going to tell you. There are exactly three roads. The first is the eye, my jewel; and if a lad has a sharp eye like yours, it's a great deal that will get into his head by that road ; you'll know a thing when you see it again, although you mayn't know your own father : that's a secret only known to your mother. The second road to larning, you spalpeen, is the ear ; and if you mind all people say, and hear all you can, you'll gain a great many truths, and just ten times as much more in the shape of lies ; you see the wheat and the chaff will come together; and you must pick the latter out of the former at any seasonable future opportunity. Now we come to the third road to larning, which is quite a different sort of road, because you see the two first give us little trouble, and we trot along almost whether we will or not ; the third and grand road is the head itself, which requires the eye and ear to help it, and two other assistants, which we call memory and application ; so you see we have the visual, then the aural, and then the mental roads, — three hard words which you don't understand, and which I sha'n't take the trouble to explain to such an animal as you are ; for I never throw away pearls to swine, as the saying is. Now then, Mr. Keene, we must come to another part of our history. As there are three

roads to larning, so there are three manes or implements by
which boys are stimulated to larn: the first is the ruler,
which you saw me shy at the thick skull of Johnny Target;
and you see'd what a rap it gave him.   Well, then, the second
is a ferule, a thing you never heard of, perhaps, but I'll
show it you; here it is," continued Mr. O'Gallagher, producing a sort of flat wooden ladle with a hole in the centre of
it, "the ruler is for the head, as you have seen: the fer
ule is for the hand.   You have seen me use the ruler: now
I'll show you what I do with the ferule.

"You, Tommy Goskin, come here, sir."

Tommy Goskin put down his book, and came up to his
master with a good deal of doubt in his countenance.

"Tommy Goskin, you didn't say your lesson well to-day."

"Yes I did, Mr. O'Gallagher," replied Tommy: "you
said I did yourself."

"Well, then. sir, you didn't say it well yesterday," continued Mr. O'Gallagher.

"Yes, I did, sir," replied the boy, whimpering.

"And is it you who dares to contradict me?" cried Mr.
O'Gallagher: "at all events, you won't say it well to-morrow; so hold out your right hand."

Poor Tommy held it out, and roared lustily at the first
blow, wringing his fingers with the smart.

"Now your left hand, sir; fair play is a jewel: always
carry the dish even."

Tommy received a blow on his left hand, which was followed up with similar demonstrations of suffering.

"There, sir, you may go now," said Mr. O'Gallagher;
"and mind you don't do it again, or else there'll be a
blow-up.   And now, Master Keene, we come to the third
and last, which is the birch for the back.   Here it is: have
you ever had a taste?"

"No, sir," replied I.

"Well, then, you have that pleasure to come; and come it
will, I don't doubt, if you and I are a few days longer acquainted.   Let me see"—

Here Mr. O'Gallagher looked round the school as if to
find a culprit; but the boys, aware of what was going on,
kept their eyes so attentively to their books, that he could
not discover one: at last he singled out a fat chubby lad.

"Walter Puddock, come here, sir."

Walter Puddock came accordingly: evidently he gave
himself up for lost.

"Walter Puddock, I have just been telling Master Keene that you're the best Latin scholar in the whole school. Now sir, don't make me out to be a liar; do me credit; or, by the blood of the O'Gallaghers, I'll flog ye till you're as thin as a herring. What's the Latin for a cocked hat, as the Roman gentlemen wore with their *togeys?*"

Walter Puddock hesitated a few seconds.

"See, now! the guilty tief! he knows what's coming; shame upon you, Walter Puddock, to disgrace your preceptor so, and make him tell a lie to young Master Keene! Where's Phil Mooney? Come along, sir, and hoist Walter Puddock; it's no larning that I can drive into you, Phil, but it's sartain sure that by your manes I drive a little into the other boys."

Walter Puddock, as soon as he was on the back of Phil Mooney, received a dozen cuts with the rod, well laid on. He bore it without flinching, although the tears rolled down his cheeks.

"There, Walter Puddock, I told you it would end in a blow-up. Go to your dictionary, you dirty blackguard, and do more credit to your education and superior instruction from a certain person who shall be nameless."

Mr. O'Gallagher laid the rod on one side, and then continued, —

"Now, Master Keene, I've just shown you the three roads to larning, and also the three implements to persuade little boys to larn: if you don't travel very fast by the three first, why, you will be followed up very smartly by the three last. A nod's as good as a wink to a blind horse, any day. And now, you've got the whole theory of the art of tuition, Master Keene: please the pigs, we'll commence with the practice to-morrow."

CAPTAIN MARRYAT.

TWO IRISH IDYLS.

RIDING DOUBLE.

Trottin' to the fair,
  Me and Moll Malony,
Seated, I declare,
  On a single pony.

How am I to know that
  Molly's safe behind,
Wid our heads in oh ! that
  Awkward way inclined ?
By her gentle breathin'
  Whispered past my ear,
And her white arms wreathin'
  Warm around me *here.*
      Trottin' to the fair,
        Me and Moll Malony,
      Seated, I declare,
        On a single pony.

Yerriz ! Masther Jack,
  Lift your fore-legs higher,
Or a rousin' crack,
  Surely you'll require.
" Oh," says Moll, " I'm frightened
  That the pony'll start ! "
And her hands she tightened
  On my happy heart;
Till widout reflectin',
  'Twasn't quite the vogue,
Somehow I'm suspectin'
  That I snatched a pogue.
      Trottin' to the fair,
        Me and Moll Malony,
      Seated, I declare,
        On a single pony.

RIDING TREBLE.

Joultin' to the fair,
  Three upon the pony,
That so lately were
  Me and Moll Malony.
" How can three be on, boy ?
  Sure the wife and you,
Though you should be *one,* boy,
  Can't be more nor *two !* "
Arrah, now then, may be,
  You've got eyes to see

That this purty baby
  Adds us up to *three.*
    Joultin' to the fair,
      Three upon the pony,
    That so lately were
      Me and Moll Malony.

Come, give over, Jack,
  Cap'rin' and curvettin'
All that's on your back
  Foolishly forgotten';
For I've tuk the notion
  One may canterin' go,
Trottin' is a notion
  I'd extind to *two:*
But to travel steady,
  Matches best wid *three,*
And we're that already,
  Mistress Moll and Me,
    Joultin' to the fair,
      Three upon the pony,
    That so lately were
      Me and Moll Malony.
                  ALFRED PERCEVAL GRAVES.

THE BROKEN PITCHER.

As beautiful Kitty one morning was tripping,
  With a pitcher of milk, from the fair of Coleraine,
When she saw me she stumbled, the pitcher it tumbled,
  And all the sweet buttermilk watered the plain.

" Oh what shall I do now ? — 'twas looking at you now!
  Sure, sure, such a pitcher I'll ne'er meet again !
'Twas the pride of my dairy : O Barney M'Cleary !
  You're sent as a plague to the girls of Coleraine."

I sat down beside her, and gently did chide her,
  That such a misfortune should give her such pain.
A kiss then I gave her; and ere I did leave her,
  She vowed for such pleasure she'd break it again.

'Twas hay-making season, — I can't tell the reason, —
   Misfortunes will never come single, 'tis plain ;
For very soon after poor Kitty's disaster
   The devil a pitcher was whole in Coleraine.

ANONYMOUS.

PADDY'S EXCELSIOR.

'TWAS growing dark so terrible fasht,
Whin through a town up the mountain there pashed
A broth of a boy, to his neck in the shnow :
As he walked, his shillelah he swung to and fro,
Saying, "It's up to the top I'm bound for to go,
     Be jabbers ! "

He looked mortial sad, and his eyes was as bright
As a fire of turf on a cowld winther night ;
And divil a word that he said could ye tell
As he opened his mouth and let out a yell, —
"It's up till the top of the mountain I'll go,
Onless covered up wid this bodthersome shnow,
     Be jabbers ! "

Through the windows he saw, as he thravelled along,
The light of the candles and fires so warm :
But a big chunk of ice hung over his head ;
Wid a shnivel and groan, "By St. Patrick ! " he said,
"It's up to the very *tip-top* I will rush,
And then if it falls it's not meself it'll crush,
     Be jabbers ! "

"Whisht a bit," said an owld man whose head was as white
As the shnow that fell down on that miserable night :
" Shure, ye'll fall in the wather, me bit of a lad ;
For the night is so dark, and the walkin' is bad."
Bedad ! he'd not lisht to a word that was said,
But he'd go till the top if he went on his head,
     Be jabbers !

A bright, buxom young girl, such as likes to be kissed,
Axed him wudn't he stop, and how *could* he resist ?

So, shnapping his fingers and winking his eye,
While shmiling upon her, he made this reply : —
" Faith, I meant to kape on till I got to the top,
But as yer shwate self has axed me, I may as well shtop.
        Be jabbers ! "

He shtopped all night and he shtopped all day,
And ye mustn't be axing whin he *did* go away ;
Fur wouldn't he be a bastely gossoon
To be lavin his darlint in the swate honeymoon ?
Whin the owld man has peraties enough and to spare,
Shure he moight as well shtay if he's comfortable there,
        Be jabbers !

                    Harper's Magazine.

THE IRISH PHILOSOPHER.

LADIES AND GINTLEMEN, — I see so many foine-lookin'
people sittin' before me, that, if you'll excuse me, I'll be
afther takin' a seat meself. You don't know me, I'm thinking, as some of yees 'ud be noddin' to me afore this. I'm a
walkin' pedestrian, a travellin' philosopher. Terry O'Mulligan's me name. I'm from Dublin, where many philosophers before me was raised and bred. Oh, philosophy is
a foine study ! I don't know any thing about it, but it's a
foine study ! Before I *kim* over I attended an important
meetin' of philosophers in Dublin ; and the discussin' and
talkin' you'd hear there about the world 'ud warm the very
heart of Socrates or Aristotle himself. Well, there was a
great many *imminent* and learned *min* there at the meetin',
and I was there too ; and while we was in the very thickest
of a heated argument, one comes to me, and says he, " Do
you know what we're talkin' about ? " — " I do," says I, " but
I don't understand yees." — " Could ye explain the sun's
motion around the earth ? " says he. " I could," says I,
" but I'd not know could you understand or not." — " Well,"
says he, " we'll see," says he. Sure'n I didn't know any thing
how to get out of it then, so I piled in ; " for," says I to
meself, " never let on to any one that you don't know any
thing, but make them believe that you do know all about
it." So says I to him, takin' up me shillelah this way (*holding a very crooked stick perpendicular*), " We'll take that

for the straight line of the earth's equator" — how's that for gehography? (*to the audience.*) Ah, that was straight till the other day I bent it in an argument. "Wery good," says he. "Well," says I, "now the sun rises in the east" (*placing the disengaged hand at the eastern end of the stick*). Well, he couldn't deny that. "And when he gets up, he

> Darts his rosy beams — Through the mornin' gleams."

Do you moind the poetry there? (*to the audience, with a smile.*) "And he keeps on risin' and risin' till he reaches his meriden." — "What's that?" says he. "His dinner-toime," says I; "sure'n that's my Latin for dinner-toime; and when he gets his dinner

> He sinks to rest — Behind the glorious hills of the west."

Oh, begorra, there's more poetry! I fale it creepin' out all over me. "There," says I, well satisfied with myself; "will that do for ye?" — "You haven't got done with him yet," says he. "Done with him!" says I, kinder mad like; "what more do you want me to do with him? Didn't I bring him from the east to the west? What more do you want?" — "Oh," says he, "you'll have to bring him back again to the east to rise next mornin'." By St. Patrick! and wasn't I near betrayin' me ignorance! Sure'n I thought there was a large family of suns, and they rise one after the other. But I gathered meself quick, and says I to him, "Well," says I, "I'm surprised you axed me that simple question; I thought any man ud know," says I, "when the sun sinks to rest in the west — when the sun" — says I. "You said that before," says he. "Well, I want to press it stronger upon you," says I. "When the sun sinks to rest in the east, — no, west, — why, he — why he waits till it grows dark, and then he goes *back in the noight-toime!*"

MARY MALONEY'S PHILOSOPHY.

"What are you singing for?" said I to Mary Maloney.

"Oh, I don't know, ma'am, without it's because my heart feels happy."

"Happy, are you, Mary Maloney? Let me see: you don't own a foot of land in the world?"

"Foot of land, is it?" she cried, with a hearty Irish laugh. "Oh, what a hand ye be after joking: why, I haven't a penny, let alone the land."

"Your mother is dead?"

"God rest her soul, yes," replied Mary Maloney, with a touch of genuine pathos: "may the angels make her bed in heaven."

"Your brother is still a hard case, I suppose?"

"Ah, you may well say that. It's nothing but drink, drink, drink, and beating his poor wife, that she is, the creature."

"You have to pay your little sister's board?"

"Sure, the bit creature; and she's a good little girl, is Hinny, willing to do whatever I axes her. I don't grudge the money what goes for that."

"You haven't many fashionable dresses either, Mary Maloney?"

"Fashionable, is it? Oh, yes, I put a piece of whalebone in my skirt, and me calico gown looks as big as the great ladies'. But then ye says true, I hasn't but two gowns to me back, two shoes to me feet, and one bonnet to me head, barring the old hood ye gave me."

"You haven't any lover, Mary Maloney?"

"Oh, be off wid ye — ketch Mary Maloney getting a lover these days, when the hard times is come. No, no, thank Heaven I haven't got that to trouble me yet, nor I don't want it."

"What on earth, then, have you got to make you happy? A drunken brother, a poor helpless sister, no mother, no father, no lover: why, where do you get all your happiness from?"

"The Lord be praised, miss, it growed up in me. Give me a bit of sunshine, a clean flure, plenty of work, and a sup at the right time, and I'm made. That makes me laugh and sing; and then, if deep trouble comes, why, God helpin' me, I'll try to keep my heart up. Sure, it would be a sad thing if Patrick McGrue should take it into his head to come an' ax me, but, the Lord willin', I'd try to bear up under it." PHILADELPHIA BULLETIN.

BRIDGET MCRAE'S WEDDING ANNIVERSARY.

HOW SHE CELEBRATED THAT SAME.

'Tis jist tin years ago, my Mike,
　Since you and me was wed;
Whin common folks make widdins like,
　Of tin or wood or lead.

In troth, we are more sinsible,
　A cosey hour to pass,
So now jist faix your gaping mouth
　For whiskey from this glass.

Yez ricolect, my darlint Mike,
　Tin years ago to-night,
Ye sware protiction till ye'd die,
　And dared the wourld to fight.

With eyes so blue, and cheeks so red,
　My face a lord might suit;
Ye vowed ye'd shoot the bla'gard through
　Who would that same dispute.

Ah, will, in troth ye say it, b'y,
　I was a han'sum girl;
So here's a glass filled to yer j'y,
　And blissings on yer sowl.

Och! mind yer, Mike, the eye yer give
　To sootherin Pat one day?
'Twas thin I give my troth to have
　My Michael McRae.

And, Mike, yer did protict me well —
　By work and batings too —
From losing heaven by spinding all
　My silly love on you.

Come, take anither glass, my b'y,
   Mysilf will drink to Pat,
For sure he had a winning way,
   And — wurrur! what is that?

Och! villain, see, ye've blacked my eye!
   I'm murthered, och! Perlice!
Shtop bating me! they'll take ye, b'y,
   For kaping not the pace.

Och! niver run, but hide yoursil'
   Here in this impty chist.
— Ah! come ye gintlemen for ill
   To Mike? he's gone out, jist!

"Yez heard a woman call," did yez?
   Shure this 's a counthrie free;
And can't a man bate what is his,
   Nor cilibrate the day?

Do now begone, ye varmint race;
   But hist! I promise ye
That Mike and me will kape the pace,
   If now ye'll let us be.

— Come out and take anither thrate,
   These gints are gone, my Mike:
Our widdin may we cilibrate
   Nixt ten years as we like.

                   Nina Gray.

PADDY O'RAFTHER.

PADDY, in want of a dinner one day,
Credit all gone, and no money to pay,
Stole from a priest a fat pullet, they say,
   And went to confession just afther.
"Your riv'rince." says Paddy, "I stole a fat hen."
"What, what!" says the priest, "at your owld thricks
   again?
Faith, you'd rather be staalin' than sayin' *amen,*
             Paddy O'Rafther!"

" Sure you wouldn't be angry," says Pat, " if you knew
That the best of intintions I had in my view;
For I stole it to make it a present to you,
　　And you can absolve me afther."
" Do you think," says the priest, " I'd partake of your theft?
Of your seven small senses you must be bereft:
You're the biggest blackguard that I know, right or left,
　　　　　　　　　　Paddy O'Rafther."

" Then what shall I do with the pullet," says Pat,
" If your riv'rince won't take it ?　By this and by that,
I don't know no more than a dog or a cat
　　What your riv'rince would have me be afther."
" Why, then," says his rev'rence, " you sin-blinded owl,
Give back to the man that you stole from, his fowl;
For, if you do not, 'twill be worse for your sowl,
　　　　　　　　　　Paddy O'Rafther."

Says Paddy, " I asked him to take it—'tis thrue
As this minit I'm talkin', your riv'rince, to you;
But he wouldn't resaive it, so what can I do ? "
　　Says Paddy, nigh chokin' with laughther.
" By my throth," says the priest, " but the case is absthruse:
If he won't take his hen, why, the man is a goose.
'Tis not the first time my advice was no use,
　　　　　　　　　　Paddy O'Rafther.

" But, for sake of your sowl, I would sthrongly advise
To some one in want you would give your supplies,—
Some widow or orphan, with tears in their eyes;
　　And *then* you may come to *me* afther."
So Paddy went off to the brisk Widow Hoy;
And the pullet, between them, was eaten with joy.
And, says she, " 'Pon my word, you're the cleverest boy,
　　　　　　　　　　Paddy O'Rafther."

Then Paddy went back to the priest the next day,
And told him the fowl he had given away
To a poor lonely widow, in want and dismay,
　　The loss of her spouse weeping afther.
" Well, now," says the priest, " I'll absolve you, my lad,
For repentantly making the best of the bad,
In feeding the hungry and cheering the sad,
　　　　　　　　　　Paddy O'Rafther."
　　　　　　　　　　　Samuel Lover.

PAT'S REASON.

ONE day, in a crowded Market-street car,
A lady was standing. She had ridden quite far,
And seemed much disposed to indulge in a frown,
As nobody offered to let her sit down.
And many there sat, who, to judge by their dress,
Might a gentleman's natural instincts possess;
But who, judged by their acts, make us firmly believe
That appearances often will sadly deceive.
There were some most intently devouring the news,
And some, through the windows, enjoying the views;
And others indulged in a make-believe nap,
While the lady stood holding on by the strap.
At last a young Irishman, fresh from the "sod,"
Arose with a smile and most comical nod,
Which said quite as plain as in words could be stated,
That the lady should sit in the place he'd vacated.
"Excuse me," said Pat, "that I caused you to wait
So long before offerin' to give you a sate;
But in truth I was only just waitin' to see
If there wasn't more gintlemin here beside me."

O'BRANIGAN'S DRILL.

THE echoes of Sumter had thrilled through the land;
And Michael O'Branigan, born to command,
Obtained a commission. A word and a nod,
And his roster was filled with the sons of "the sod."
It is true that his knowledge of tactics was scant:
When he wished to "oblique," his command would be,
        "Slant!"
But he knew the importance of practical skill;
And, marching his company out to a hill,
Proceeded with this introductory drill:—

"Attintion! Right driss! Be that token is meant
That aich of ye keeps his nixt neighbor fernint.
Shtand up like meself, an' look martial an' brave
Wid a souldierly bearin'!—Mulcahey, ye knave,
Don't ye offer to shtep from the ranks till ye've lave.

"Attintion!   Fix bayonets!   Jisht for the drill,
We will play that the foe is a-houldin' the hill.
Now, double-quick!   Charge!   An' I'll lade the **way**;
An' this is yer watchword — fwhat is it?   Hooray!
Attintion!   Ha — halt, till I come till me breath!
Give O'Branigan time, an' he'll lade ye till death!
Halt, Rafferty, Lafferty!   Wait till I come!
Shtand shtill an' marrk time till the bate of the drum!
It isn't the rulable usage of war
To follow yer captain, unless he's before.

"Attintion!   To prove to our foemen their folly,
We'll load up our rifles an' give them a volley;
An' to show how composed a bould souldier can shtand,
I will shtep to the front while I give the command.
Make ready!   Take aim!   Patsy, point your gun higher!
Don't shut the wrong eye whin ye're aimin' it.   Fire!

"Oh!   Murther!   I'm kilt! — Sargint Murphy, ye brute,
Don't ye know, whin ye ounly blank cartridges shoot,
If yer ramrod ye happen to lave in yer gun
It's more deadly than forty-two bullets in one?
Jisht look at me hat, wid its horrible rint,
An' its iligant aigle to smithereens sint!
Ye're arrishted!   Moind that, now!   Ye'll pay for yer guilt!
I'd 'av' hung ye for murther, an I had been kilt.
Faix, ye're sargint, to-day, of the guard, Murphy!   Whisht!
Go report till yersilf as put undher arrisht!"

So closed the first drill; but he proved, when the field
In the chaos of jarring artillery reeled,
That, to quote a plain soldier's description, "So far
As concerns the tough tussle and business of war,
O'Branigan's flannel-mouthed veterans were *there*."

                                        W. W. Fink.

-----◆-----

PAT AND THE PIG.

WE have read of a Pat so financially flat,
     That he had neither money nor meat,
And when hungry and thin, it was whispered by sin,
     That he ought to steal something to eat.

So he went to the sty of a widow near by,
  And he gazed on the tenant — poor soul!
" Arrah now," said he, " what a trate that'll be,"
  And the pig of the widow he stole.

In a feast he rejoiced; then he went to a judge,
  For in spite of the pork and the lard,
There was something within, that was sharp as a pin.
  For his conscience was pricking him hard.

And he said with a tear, " Will your Riverence hear
  What I have in sorrow to say? "
Then the story he told, and the TALE did unfold
  Of the pig he had taken away.

And the judge to him said, " Ere you go to your bed
  You must pay for the pig you have taken,
For 'tis thus, by me sowl, you'll be saving your sowl,
  And will also be saving your bacon."

" Oh, be jabers," said Pat, " I can niver do that —
  Not the ghost of a hap'orth have I —
And I'm wretched indade if a penny it nade
  Any pace for me conscience to buy."

Then in sorrow he cried, and the judge he replied,
  " Only think how you'll tremble with fear
When the judge you shall meet at the great judgment seat,
  And the widow you plundered while here."

" Will the widow be there? " whispered Pat with a stare,
  " And the pig? by my sowl, is it true? "
" They will surely be there," said the judge, " I declare,
  And, oh Paddy! what then will you do? "

" Many thanks," answered Pat, " for you telling me that,
  May the blessings upon you be big!
On that settlemint day, to the widow I'll say,
  Mrs. Flannegan, here is your pig! "

PAT AND THE OYSTERS.

ONE evening a red-headed Connaught swell, of no small aristocratic pretensions in his own eyes, sent his servant, whom he had just imported from the long-horned kingdom, in all the rough majesty of a creature fresh from the " wilds," to purchase a hundred of oysters on the City Quay. Paddy staid so long away, that Squire Trigger got quite impatient and unhappy, lest his "body man" might have slipped into the Liffey. However, to his infinite relief, Paddy soon made his appearance, puffing and blowing like a disabled bellows, but carrying his load seemingly in great triumph. " Well, Pat," cried the master, "what the devil kept you so long ? " — " Long! Ah, thin, maybe it's what you'd have me to come home with half my *arrant?* " says Pat. " Half the oysters ? " says the master. " No ; but too much of the *fish*," says Pat. " What fish? " says he. " The oysters, to be sure," says Pat. " What do you mean, blockhead ? " says he. " I mean," says Pat, "that there was no use in loading myself with more nor was useful." — " Will you explain yourself ? " says he. " I will," says Pat, laying down his load. "Well, then, you see, plaise your honor, as I was coming home along the quay, mighty peaceable, who should I meet but Shammus Maginus? ' Good-morrow, Shamien,' sis I. ' Good-morrow, kindly, Paudeen,' sis he. ' What is it you have in the sack? ' sis he. ' A hundred of oysters,' sis I. ' Let us look at them,' sis he. ' I will, and welcome,' sis I. ' Arrah! thunder and pratees! ' sis he, opening the sack, and examinin' them, ' who *sowld* you these? ' — ' One Tom Kinahan that keeps a small ship there below,' sis I. ' Musha, then, bad luck to that same Tom that *sowld* the likes to you! ' sis he. ' Arrah! why, avick ? ' sis I. ' To make a *bolsour* ov you, an' give them to you without claning thim,' sis he. ' An' arn't they claned, Jim, aroon ? ' sis I. — ' Oh! bad luck to the one of thim,' sis he. ' Musha then,' says I, ' what the dhoul will I do at all, at all? fur the master will be mad.' — ' Do! ' sis he, ' why, I'd rather do the thing for you mysel, nor you should lose your place,' sis he. So wid that he begins to clane them wid his knife, *nate* and *well* , an', afeered ov dirtying the flags, begor, he swallowed the insides hisself from beginnin' to ind, tal he had them as dacent as you see thim here," dashing down at his master's feet his bag of oyster-shells, to his master's no small amazement.

A PENITENT.

ARRAH, Nora, don't look like a thunder-cloud darlint:
What harm if I did stale a kiss from your lips?
No sinsible bee meets a smiling young rose, sure,
But stops, the sly thafe, and a honey-drop sips.
And, rose of the wurruld, spake aisy now, ain't I
More sinsible far than a vagabond bee?
And how could I see the swate kiss that was lying
There on your red lips, as though waiting for me,
And not take it, darlint?   Och, Nora, give o'er!
Faith, I'm awful sorry — *I didn't take more.*

'Twas your fault, intirely.   Why did you smile at me?
So great a timptation no man could resist,
For your laughing blue eyes, and your cheeks wid a dimple,
And your dilicate mouth said, " We're here to be kissed."
And could I be dreaming they didn't spake truth, dear —
Sure beautiful fatures like thim never lie;
If they do you should hide them, and not be desaving
Such an innocent, trusting young fellow as I.
Are you frowning still, darlint?   Och, Nora, give o'er!
Don't I tell you I'm sorry — *I didn't take more?*

MARGARET EYTINGE.

MIKE McGAFFATY'S DOG.

MICHAEL McGAFFATY — faith, what a name,
    Was an Irishman born, and an Irishman bred.
His brogue was as broad as his brawny frame,
    And his hands were as thick as his carroty head.

Mike had a wife who was Erin's true child,
    Red-headed, big-fisted, and ugly was she;
Her features were fierce, and her nature not mild,
    And she was as stupid as stupid could be.

And Mike had a dog, a bristling young terrier,
    Quick at a fight, and not slow at a bone;
In the family-circle none could be merrier,
    But he'd howl like a dervish when left all alone.

Mike lived in a hovel, untidy and small,
  One room for two persons is found not too big:
Two persons, I said? Now, faith, that's not all,
  For the cosiest corner was kept for the pig.

Now, with Mike, and his wife, and the pig and the dog,
  While none disagreed, all was quiet and right;
But a quarrel arose, 'twixt the cur and the hog,
  And one night they set to and indulged in a fight.

Then Biddy loud stormed, and louder Mike swore,
  The pig squealed and grunted, the dog yelled like mad;
So to make everything quiet and peaceful once more,
  Mike turned out the dog and then quiet was had.

But the dog was unused to the cold and the snow,
  Did not take his ejectment quite in good part;
Not a step from the door would the ugly cur go,
  But sat there and howled till the hut seemed to start.

Again Biddy loud stormed, and louder Mike swore,
  While the pig sweetly slept, quite free from all care;
And Mike must get up from his slumbers once more,
  To stop the wronged terrier's musical air.

He rushed to the doorway in anger and wrath,
  Ne'er stopping for clothing, as quickly he bowled;
There sat the scared terrier right in his path,
  Awakening the echoes as loudly he howled.

The door was banged to, leaving Biddy alone,
  The howling was hushed and stillness restored;
Bolt upright sat Biddy, now Michael was gone,
  While " in slumbers of midnight " the pig loudly snored.

So long was he gone that his spouse was alarmed,
  She moved from her bed and peeped out at the door;
For rather than have her McGaffaty harmed,
  She'd endure this dog's howling and that of ten more.

The moon glistens brightly on hillocks of snow,
  And there, in a deep drift, stands Mike and the cur;
O'er his half-naked form the chilling winds blow,
  Like a statue the dog stands, not daring to stir.

In wonder she gazes on human and brute,
  Such a sight never met mortal eyes, I declare;
From Mike's ears and his nose long icicles stood,
  While a small drift of snow rises white in his hair.

In the heart of fair Biddy anger is brewing,
  And her shrilly pitched voice of panic doth smack;
"Mike! Mike! you big blackguard, what now be ye doing,
  Sweating there in the could wid no coat to yer back?

Mike turned at the voice of his blooming young daisy,
  While in shivering accents he answered in haste,
"Whist, Biddy! my darling, now can't yer be aisy,
  Don't yer see what I'm doing? I'm frazing the baste."

"'Tis frazing the baste is it?" answered fair Biddy,
  As into the hut she indignantly burst;
"If yer stay there much longer you'll leave me a widdy,
  For in frazing the brute you will fraze yerself first."

MARK MELVILLE.

JIMMY BUTLER AND THE OWL.

AN IRISH STORY.

'TWAS in the summer of '46 that I landed at Hamilton, fresh as a new pratie just dug from the "ould sod," and wid a light heart and a heavy bundle I sot off for the township of Buford, tiding a taste of a song, as merry a young fellow as iver took the road. Well, I trudged on and on, past many a plisant place, pleasin' meself wid the thought that some day I might have a place of me own, wid a world of chickens and ducks and pigs and childer about the door; and along in the afternoon of the sicond day I got to Buford village. A cousin of me mother's, one Dennis O'Dowd, lived about siven miles from there, and I wanted to make his place that night; so I inquired the way at the tavern, and was lucky to find a man who was goin' part of the way, and would show me the way to find Dennis. Sure he was very kind indade, an' when I got out of his wagon, he pointed me through the wood, and tould me to go straight south a mile and a half, an' the first house would be Dennis's.

"An' you've no time to lose, now," said he, "for the sun is low; an' mind you don't get lost in the woods."

"Is it lost, now," said I, "that I'd be gittin', an' me uncle as great a navigator as iver steered a ship across the thrackless say! Not a bit of it, though I'm obleeged to ye for your kind advice, and thank yiz for the ride."

'An' wid that he drove off an' left me alone. I shouldered me bundle bravely, an', whistlin' a bit of tune for company like, I pushed into the bush. Well, I went a long way over bogs, an' turnin' round among the bush an' trees till I began to think I must be well-nigh to Dennis's. But, bad 'cess to it! all of a sudden I came out of the woods at the very identical spot where I started in, which I knew by an ould crotched tree that seemed to be standin' on its head an' kickin' up its heels to make divarsion of me. By this time it was growin' dark, and as there war no time to lose, I started in a second time, determined to keep straight south this time, and no mistake. I got on bravely for a while; but och hone! och hone! it got so dark I couldn't see the trees, an' I bumped me nose an' barked me shins, while the miskaties bit me hands an' face to a blister; an' after tumblin' an' stumblin' around till I was fairly bamfoozled, I sat down on a log, all of a trimble, to think that I was lost intirely, an' that maybe a lion, or some other wild crayther, would devour me before mornin'.

Just then I heard somebody a long way off say, "Whip poor Will!" "Bedad!" sez I, "I'm glad it isn't Jamie that's got to take it, though it seems it's more in sorrow than in anger they are doin' it, or why should they say 'poor Will'? an' sure they can't be Injin, haythin, or naygur, for it's plain English they're afther spakin'. Maybe they might help me out o' this;" so I shouted, at the top of my voice, "A lost man!" Thin I listened. Prisently an answer came:

"Who! whoo! Whooo!"

"Jamie Butler, the waiver!" sez I, as loud as I could roar; an' snatchin' up my bundle an' stick, I started in the direction of the voice. Whin I thought I had got near the place, I stopped and shouted again: "A lost man!"

"Who! whoo! whooo!" said a voice right over my head.

"Sure," thinks I, "it's a mighty quare place for a man to be at this time of night; maybe it's some settler scrapin' sugar off a sugar-bush, for the children's breakfast in the mornin'. But where's Will, and the rest of them?" All this wint through me head like a flash; and thin I answered his inquiry:

"Jamie Butler, the waiver," sez I; "an' if it wouldn't inconvanience yer honor, would yiz be kind enough to step down an show me the way to the house of Dennis O'Dowd?"

"Who! whoo! whooo!" sez he.

"Dennis O'Dowd!" sez I, civil enough; "and a dacent man he is, and first cousin to me own mother."

"Who! whoo! whooo!" sez he again.

"Me mother!" says I; "and as fine a woman as iver peeled a biled pratie wid her thumb-nail; and her maiden name was Molly McFiggin."

"Who! whoo! whooo!"

"Paddy McFiggin! bad luck to yer deaf ould head,—Paddy McFiggin, I say—do ye hear that? An' he was the tallest man in all the county Tipperary, excipt Jim Doyle, the black-smith."

"Who! whoo! whooo!"

"Jim Doyle, the blacksmith!" sez I, "ye good-for-nothin' blaggurd naygur, and if yiz don't come down and show me the way this min't, I'll climb up there and break ivry bone in your skin, ye spalpeen, so sure as me name is Jimmy Butler!"

"Who! whoo! whooo!" says he, as impident as iver.

I said niver a word, but layin' down me bundle, and takin' me stick in me teeth, I began to climb the tree. Whin I got among the branches, I looked quietly around till I saw a pair of big eyes just forninst me.

"Whist," sez I, "an' I'll let him have a taste of an Irish stick;" an' wid that I let drive an' lost me balance an' came tumblin' to the ground, nearly breakin' me neck wid the fall. Whin I came to me sinsis I had a very sore head, wid a lump on it like a goose-egg, and half of me Sunday coat-tail torn off intirely. I spoke to the chap in the tree, but could git niver an answer at all, at all.

"Sure," thinks I, "he must have gone home to rowl up his head, for, by the powers, I didn't throw me stick for nothin'."

Well, by this time the moon was up, an' I could see a little, an' I detarmined to make one more effort to reach Dennis's.

I wint on cautiously for a while, an' thin I heard a bell. "Sure," sez I, "I'm comin' to a settlement now, for I hear the church-bell." I kept on toward the sound till I came to an ould cow wid a bell on. She started to run; but I was too quick for her, an' got her by the tail an' hung on, thinkin' that maybe she would take me out of the woods. On we wint, like an ould-country steeple-chase, till, sure enough, we came out to a clearin' an' a house in sight wid a light in it. So, leavin' the ould cow puffin' an' blowin' in a shed, I wint to the

house, an', as luck would have it, whose should it be but
Dennis's?

He gave me a raal Irish welcome, an' introduced me to his
two daughters — as purty a pair of girls as iver ye clapped an eye
on. But whin I tould him me adventure in the woods, an' about
the fellow who made fun of me, they all laughed an' roared, an'
Dennis said it was an owl.

"An ould what?" sez I.

"Why, an owl, a bird," sez he.

"Do ye tell me now?" sez I. "Sure, it's a quare country
and a quare bird."

An' thin they all laughed again, till at last I laughed meself
that hearty like, an' dropped right into a chair between the two
purty girls; an' the ould chap winked at me, an' roared again.

Dennis is me father-in-law now, an' he often yet delights to
tell our childer about their daddy's adventure wid the owl.

ANONYMOUS

TIPPERARY.

These lines are said to have been addressed to a Dr. Fitzgerald, on reading
the following couplet in his apostrophe to his native village: —

"And thou! dear village, loveliest of the clime,
  Fain would I name thee, but I'm scant in rhyme."

A BARD there was in sad quandary,
To find a rhyme for Tipperary.
Long labored he through January,
Yet found no rhyme for Tipperary;
Toiled every day in February,
But toiled in vain for Tipperary;
Searched Hebrew text and commentary,
But searched in vain for Tipperary;
Bored all his friends at Inverary,
To find a rhyme for Tipperary;
Implored the aid of " Paddy Carey,"
Yet still no rhyme for Tipperary;
He next besought his mother Mary,
To tell him rhyme for Tipperary;

But she, good woman, was no fairy,
Nor witch — though born in Tipperary;
Knew every thing about her dairy,
But not the rhyme for Tipperary;
The stubborn Muse he could not vary,
For still the lines would run contrary,
Whene'er he thought on Tipperary;
And though of time he was not chary,
'Twas thrown away on Tipperary;
Till, of his wild-goose chase most weary,
He vowed to leave out Tipperary;
But, no: the theme he might not vary,
His longing was not temporary,
To find meet rhyme for Tipperary;
He sought among the gay and airy,
He pestered all the military,
Committed many a strange vagary,
Bewitched, it seemed, by Tipperary.
He wrote post-haste to Darby Leary,
Besought with tears his Auntie Sairie,
But sought he far, or sought he near, he
Ne'er found a rhyme for Tipperary.
He travelled sad through Cork and Kerry,
He drove "like mad" through sweet Dunbary,
Kicked up a precious tantar-ara,
But found no rhyme for Tipperary;
Lived fourteen weeks at Straw-ar-ara,
Was well-nigh lost in Glenègary,
Then started "slick" for Demerara,
In search of rhyme for Tipperary.
Through "Yankee-land," sick, solitary,
He roamed by forest, lake, and prairie—
He went *per terrem et per mare* —
But found no rhyme for Tipperary.
Through orient climes on dromedary,
On camel's back through great Sahara—
His travels were extraordinary —
In search of rhyme for Tipperary.
Fierce as a gorgon or chimæra,
Fierce as Alecto or Megæra,
Fiercer than e'er a love-sick bear, he
Raged through "the londe" of Tipperary;
His cheeks grew thin, and wondrous hairy,

His visage long, his aspect "eerie,"
His *tout ensemble*, faith! 'twould scare ye,
Amidst the wilds of Tipperary.
Becoming hypochon-dri-ary,
He sent for his apothecary,
Who ordered "balm" and saponary,—
Herbs rare to find in Tipperary.
In his potations ever wary,
His choicest drink was "home gooseberry."
On swipes, skim-milk, and smallest beer, he
Scanted rhyme for his Tipperary.
Had he imbibed good old Madeira,
Drank "pottle-deep" of golden sherry,
Of Falstaff sack, or ripe canary,
No rhyme had lacked for Tipperary.
Or had his tastes been literary,
He might have found extemporary,
Without the aid of dictionary,
Some fitting rhyme for Tipperary.
Or had he been an antiquary,
Burnt midnight oil in his library,
Or been of temper less "camsteary,"
Rhymes had not lacked for Tipperary.
He paced about his aviary,
Blew up sky-high his secretary,
And then in truth and anger sware he,
There was no rhyme for Tipperary.

PAT'S DREAM OF HEAVEN.

I DHREAMED I wint to hivin one night,
    And knocked at the big white gate,
And the good St. Peter he opened it,
    But he towld me I'd have to wait
While he looked for me name in the howly book;
    And whin he had found it there,
He bade me come in, though he towld me plain
    That min comin' that way was rare.

I axed him how was business now;
  And he twirled the golden kay,
And answered he had very little to do,
  So few ever came that way.
So I shtopped a bit to chat wid him,
  And I axed could I took around:
He said, " Oh, yes! as ye've once got in,
  Yer free to the whole uv the ground.

  " Free to walk by the river uv life,
  To rist in the mansions of light,
To shtand in the timple not made by hands,
  Wid the sunbhurst uv glory bright."
I seen the apostles a-mindin' their nets,
  And I axed what need uv um now;
And the howliest light shone round about
  Each howly apostle's brow
As they answered, " Our nets must be strong indeed,
  To draw min's souls away
From the bogs of doubt they are clingin' in,
  To the light uv perfect day."

I saw the martyrs of olden time,
  The saints and angels fair,
And millions and millions uv young spalpeens
  All playing together there;
And Mary the Mother wid love in her eyes
  Looked down on each little child;
And the blessed Teacher was teachin' them,
  So gentle and undefiled.

But away in a corner I heard a noise:
  I thought 'twas a bit uv a row;
So I loosed my shillelah. "Begorra!" says I,
  "If it's fightin' I'll jest show um how."
But whin I dhrew nearer I heard them shpake,
  And they was a-tellin' aloud
The story of Joseph the carpenter,
  To a listenin' bit of a crowd.

Now, Joseph, it seems, was a good-natured sowl,
  And what he was towld he believed;
And many's the frind, on his recommind,
  By Peter had been received.

But Peter at last found this wouldn't do:
  So he towld to the carpenter Joe
That no more frinds in his recommind
  Inside the gate should go.

Then what does Joseph the carpenter do,
  But, bein' so deft at his trade,
He wint to work wid hammer and plane,
  And a long, shtrong ladder he made;
And thrusting it out of window high,
  'Fore they knowed what he was about,
He was snakin' his frinds by the dozens in,
  And that was what made the rout.

And Paul the preacher, the earnest heart,
  Had found out what was goin' on ;
And he was tellin' the story strange
  To Matthew, Mark, and John.
And Peter the doorkaper left his place,
  And drew near and listened too;
And he waxed very wroth. "Now, Joseph," says he,
  " I've had too much trouble wid you.

" Let me hear no more of these wicked pranks,
  Or we'll have a council of war,
And see if there's no makin' you
  Abide by the common law.
We will have you cast out as an inemy, —
  The dhragon was long ago, —
And then you must wander a thousand years
  In darkness and death, you know."

Now, Joseph the carpenter bowed, and said,
  " Is it turnin' me out, ye mane?
Shure I'll go at once, if you think it best,
  And niver a word I'll complain :
But a man has a right to his family."
  Here he winked his eye and shmiled.
" And 'twould break up your whole institution, shure,
  If I took my wife and her Child."

And all the apostles took up their nets,
  And silently walked away;
And Peter moved off scratchin' his ear
  Wid the end uv the golden kay;
And Joseph the carpenter whistled a tune.
  I thought 'twas a bit of a joke,
But I feared to laugh, so I made up my mind
  'Twas all a dhrame — and I woke.

BIDDY'S TROUBLES.

"IT's thru for me, Katy, that I never seed the like of this
people afore. It's a sorry time I've been having since coming to this house, twelve months agone this week Thursday.
Yer knew, honcy, that my fourth coosin, Ann Macarthy,
recommended me to Mrs. Whaler, and told the lady that I
knew about ginteel housework and the likes; while at the
same time I had niver seed inter an American lady's
kitchen. So she engaged me, and my heart was jist ready
to burst wid grief for the story that Ann had told, for Mrs.
Whaler was a swate-spoken lady, and never looked cross-
like in her life; that I knew by her smooth kind face. Well,
jist the first thing she told me to do, after I dressed the children, was to dress the ducks for dinner. I stood looking at
the lady for a couple of minutes, before I could make out
any meaning at all to her words. Thin I went searching
after clothes for the ducks; and such a time as I had to be
sure. High and low I went, till at last my mistress axed
me for what I was looking; and I told her the clothes for the
ducks, to be sure. Och, how she scramed and laughed, till
my face was as rid as the sun wid shame, and she showed me
in her kind swate way what her meaning was. Thin she told
me how to air the beds; and it was a day for me, indade,
when I could go up chamber alone and clare up the rooms.
One day Mrs. Whaler said to me, —

"'Biddy, an' ye may give the baby an airin', if yees
will.'

"What should I do — and it's thru what I am saying this
blessed minute — but go up stairs wid the child, and shake

it, and then howld it out of the winder. Such a screaming
and kicking as the baby gave — but I hild on the harder.
Everybody thin in the strate looked up at me; at last misthress came up to see what for was so much noise.

" ' I am thrying to air the baby,' I said, ' but it kicks and
scrames dridfully.'

" 'There was company down below; and whin Mrs. Whaler told them what I had been after doing, I thought they
would scare the folks in the strate wid scraming.

" And then I was told I must do up Mr. Whaler's sharts
one day when my mistress was out shopping.   She told
me repeatedly to do them up nice, for master was going
away; so I takes the sharts and did them all up in some
paper that I was after bringing from the ould counthry wid
me, and tied some nice pink ribbon around the bundle.

" ' Where are the sharts, Biddy?' axed Mrs. Whaler,
when she comed home.

" ' I have been doing them up in a quair nice way,' I said,
bringing her the bundle.

" ' Will you iver be done wid your graneness?' she axed
me with a loud scrame.

" I can't for the life of me be tellin' what their talkin'
manes.   At home we call the likes of this fine work starch-
ing; and a deal of it I have done, too.   Och! and may the
blessed vargin pity me, for I never'll be cured of my graneness!''

"MAKE IT FOUR, YER HONOR."

Was ye iver in coort av a mornin',
　　When the shiverin' sinners come,
Like bastes from their iron cages,
　　To be tould their guilt and doom?
Some av thim bould and brazen,
　　Some av thim broke wid care,
Some av thim wild and wapin',
　　Or sullen wid black despair.

Oh! it's a sight inthirely
　　To take the heart away, —
The pitiful little children,
　　The ould ones dirthy and gray;

Crouchin' along the benches,
  Tuckin' their rags about,
To hide the sorrow that's in thim,
  And kape the couldness out.

There is the Judge above thim,
  The coort's own officers;
Police, wid their long shillelahs,
  Nate in their coats and stars.
Witnesses, too, a plinty;
  Shysters to worry and bite,
And, hangin' about the railin',
  The divil's own crew for fight.

Nine av the clock is sthrikin'
  When the clark begins to read,
An' prisintly his Honor
  Says to the coort, "Proceed."
Thin up they call ould Mary,
  And thrimblin' there she stands:
The comb's forgotten that's felt her hair,
  An' the soap that's seen her hands.

Larry, my boy, where are ye,
  That came fram ould Galway,
An' brought in yer arms a darlin',
  The swatest that crossed the say?
Could you see her now, all faded,
  In her rags and sin and shame,
Yer heart it would break wid sorrow
  That iver she bore yer name.

Then up spakes the Judge; an' says he,
  "Mary, I've seen ye here,
How many times, can ye tell me,
  Since it was the last new year?
Ye're scarcely quit av the prisin,
  And here ye are the-day,
'For sthaling,' says the witness:
  Now, what have ye to say?"

Shakin' her gray hairs backward
  Out of her eyes and face:
"It's thrue that ye say, yer Honor,
  And it's thrue it's my disgrace.

But it wasn't the coat I cared for:
  It's shtarvin' I was to eat;
And I want a Christian shilter
  Out av a Christless street.

"Sind me back to prisin;
  For the winter it is cold,
And there isn't a heart that's warmin'
  For the likes of me that's old.
There isn't a heart that's warmin',
  Nor a hand that takes me in:
If I shtale to keep from shtarvin',
  May God forgive the sin!"

Thin kindly spakes his Honor:
  "Well, Mary, will it do
If I sind you to the prisin
  For jist a month or two?"
"The jail's a friend," says Mary;
  "I fear the winther more:
If ye pity me, yer Honor,
  Ye'll plaze to make it four."

Anon.

THE POST-BOY.

"Come over the bridge, Kitty Clooney, an' up by the Black
  Rock way.
I'm going to meet the post-boy, — he's makin' his rounds to-
  day, —
An' I'll hold ye anything, Kitty, he'll bring me a bit of a note,
For my heart is singin' an' dancin' an' pumpin' up in my
  throat.

"Make haste, dear, an' throw on yer shoulders yer little red-
  hooded cloak,
For the sky hangin' over the hill-tops is heavy with clouds
  like smoke.
'Twill be only a shower I'm thinkin', for, back of the mist,
  the sun
'Tis waitin' to laugh at the mountains for thinkin' the day
was done.

"Sure, 'tis well we're two hearty colleens, not hurt by a
    sprinklin' o' rain.
If 'twas ladies was in it, Kitty, how quick they'd turn back
    again,
An' miss all the soft sweet mornin', the stretch o' the climbin'
    road,
An' the blackbird that sings in the hedges, so thick with the
    hawthorn sowed.

"The water was coolin' and fresh, then, an' curled 'round
    our feet when they stepped
From one big black stone to the next with a gurglin' splash;
    an' we've kept
Our mantles tidy and dry, or they'd tell on us over to
    home.
So we'll sit here an' rest for a minute : 'tis this way the post
    will come.

"Ah, Kitty, what do you think now? Will he bring me a
    word this day,
From my Patrick, *ma bouchal deelish*, my lad that went over
    the say
To the terrible wars an' the fightin' in the great big sorrow-
    ful land,
Where agin' one another in battle own brothers are liftin'
    the hand?

"Sure he wrote me the whole dark story, an' how from the
    very first
He went to the fight full-hearted to stand by the bitter
    worst.
I'll read ye the letter, Kitty, for I keep it still in my
    breast :
I'd no more lave it *out* than the linnet would push her young
    from the nest.

"'Not 'list! is it, Mary? he's sayin'—'Ah! 'twasn't yourself
    that spoke,
For your sweet lips would scorn the message, tho' the tender
    heart of you broke.
You'd rather grow white with the grievin' than blush at the
    coward's name
That 'ud follow me like a shadow if I sold my soul into
    shame.

"' To the shame on the son of Erin who'd turn in her grief
and need,
From the land that has welcome kind, without favor of
clime or creed,
For the millions that come in crowds from the grudgin' old
mother soil
To the country free-hearted an' flowin' with plenty for
honest toil.'

" 'Tis true, Kitty dear, 'twas fightin' for what there's no room
for here, —
The struggle for right and for freedom, that's costin' the big
world dear.
Sure the sweet Holy Mother laned smilin', and heard ev'ry
prayer that I said,
An' never let baynet or bullet touch one hair of his darlin'
head.

"Och, Kitty! I hear the post-boy! my heart with terror
faints!
If he *hasn't* a letter, Kitty! Run up while I pray to the
saints;
An' I'll shut my eyes till ye bring me the hope or the heart-
break down, —
The word that'll call me to meet him, or the silence that
laves me alone."

" Look up then, Mary Alanna! " called Kitty, as down out of
breath
She ran, where the waiting colleen sat quiet and pale as
death.
"It is not a letter, agra! but "—" Your Patrick's own self,
in troth,
That the post has brought ye to-day, Mary, — myself an' the
letter both!

" Aye, cry with the joy, *acushla*, 'twill ease your flutterin'
heart,
While I tell you over and over, we never again need part:
While I press you tight to my breast, darlin', the breast that
kept strong an' true;
For the saints in the thick of the fight, dear, were shieldin'
me safe for you!

"Come up the road now: the post-boy is waitin' the news
    to hear.
'Tis seldom he brings a letter that spakes out its mind so clear,
Or one that the givin' up of will lighten so much the load
Of that broth of a post-boy that travels along the Killarney
    road." MRS. C. J. DESPARD.

THAT FIRE AT THE NOLANS'.

IT would have been evident to even the most careless and
unobservant passer-by, that something had happened at the
Nolans'. Not that there was any thing the matter with the
house, for it bore no trace of disaster; but there were many
signs which in Shantytown betoken either a fight, a funeral,
or a fire. The Nolan mansion was the only building within six blocks that was built on the level of the street; it
was, moreover, constructed of brick, and three stories high;
decorated paper shades adorned its windows, and its door
was emblazoned with a silver plate on which were the
words, " Terence O'C. Nolan." On the particular morning
in question, all the occupants of the surrounding white-
washed, patched, and propped-up shanties were gathered on
the sidewalk in front of it. From the centre window in the
second story, Thomas-à-Becket Nolan, aged four years, with
his nose flattened against the glass, peered down at the
excited groups below. Now and then he would breathe on
the pane, and then draw strange characters over its misty
surface with his small finger. He was the unconscious
object of many remarks.

Old Mrs. Murphy, the centre of an interested knot of neighbors, was listened to with great respect because she had just
come from within the house. Michael Coogan, presuming
on the fact that he had married a sister of Dennis O'Connor,
who was Mrs. Nolan's great-uncle, ascended the steps, and
rang the bell.

"Stip in, Mr. Coogan," said Mrs. Nolan. "Good marnin'
to yer. I suppose it's askin' afther Tirry ye are, an' the
foire. Jist walk this way an' contimplate the destrooction."

"The *débree* ain't so much as removed from the flure,"
she explained as she held open the parlor door and allowed
Mr. Coogan to survey the wreck inside the room. Everything in the apartment was broken, and soaked with water;

but strangely enough there were no stains of smoke or any other trace of fire to be seen. Pictures and ornaments were all completely demolished, and broken glass covered everything.

"Howly saints!" ejaculated Mr. Coogan, "phat an ixpinsive catashtrophe, Mrs. Nolan! It's a tirrible dimonstration yez must have had."

"Ah, that it wuz," she replied, sinking into a damp and mutilated rocking-chair. "Ter think of that bee-utiful Axminister carpet, an' those impoorted Daggystan roogs, an' our new Frinch mantel clock that had the gooldfish globe over it — all soppin' wet, an' shmashed to shmithereens. It 'ud be a tremingious calamity for anybody."

"Tremingious!" echoed Mr. Coogan in an awe-struck tone, "that it wud. An' how did the occurince evintuate, Mrs. Nolan?"

"It wuz all along av the new domistic an' those divilish greeners," began Mrs. Nolan in a somewhat agitated manner, shaking her head sadly. "Lasht wake, Katy, our ould gurrel that had bin wid us fer noine years, married a longshoreman, an' so I ingaged a domistic be the name af Mary Ann Reilly. She had lost two fingers aff av her lift hand, an' wuz rid-hidded an' pock-marked, but she wuz will ricommended, an' so I tuk her at oncet. Tirry didn't loike the looks af her, at all, at all   'Bridget,' sez he, 'her eyes are not shtraight,' sez he. 'I don't like google-eyed paple in the house,' sez he. 'Look out, or she'll be afther lookin' at ye or at Tummy, an' bewitchin' ye wid her ayvil eye,' sez he. But wud ye belave me, Mr. Coogan, she only looked crucked whin she wuz narvous or excoited, and *ginerally* her eyes wuz as shtraight as yer own in yer hid. She hadn't bin in the house over two days, d'ye moind, whin I dropped the flat-oiron on me fut, scalded me hand, an' broke two chiney dishes in wan mornin', and that same day Tommy got inter the kitchen an' eat up three pounds of raishons, an' wuz shriekin' wid epleptic convulsions all noight; so I began ter put some faith in her bewitchment mesilf."

"Roight for ye," said Mr. Coogan, nodding approvingly at Mrs. Nolan. "That wuz bad loock enough, so it was."

"Will, that wuz only the beginnin'," continued Mrs. Nolan. "The nixt thing wuz yisterday mornin' whin Tirry cum home wid a bashkit full o' little, round, green bottles. 'Phat's thim?' sez I. 'Is it Christmas-tree toys, or is it

patent midicine?'—'Nayther,' sez Tirry; 'it's a family foire
departmint,' sez he. 'Since we have no tilegraft in the
house,' sez he, 'an' insoorance is so expinsible, I've bin afthor
buyin' some han' greenades ter put out foires wid.'—'Is it
limonade is in 'em, did yer say?' sez I. 'No,' sez he.
'They're greenades, Bridget. The bottles is green, an' they
aid ye ter put out a foire,' sez he. So Tirry hung up wan
dozen bottles in the parlor near the dure (where that woire
rack is, Mr. Coogan), an' instroocted Mary Ann how to ix-
tinguish foires wid thim, by trowin' thim at the flames."

"Is it base-ball that it is?" inquired Mr. Coogan.

"No, loike stonin' goats, more," said Mrs. Nolan, and then
she resumed her narrative. "Lasht avenin', the lamp wuz
lit on the table, Tummy wuz playin' by the winder, an' me
husband wuz takin' his convanience in his arrum-chair, wid
his back to the dure. *I* wuz sittin' near the table a-readin'
the mornin' *Hurruld*, an' Tummy all av a suddent lit the
winder-shade run up near the top. 'Mudder,' sez he, 'the
b'yes have made a big bonfoire in the lot opposite,' sez he.
An' from where I sat I could see the reflixion av a blazin'
tar-barrel in the loockin'-glass over the mantelpace. Jist
thin, the dure opined behind me, and Mary Ann come in.
She saw the reflixion too, an' yelled, '*Foire!*' loike bloody
murder. I turns round to look at her, and she wuz trimblin'
wid oxcoitemint, an' as google-eyed as a crab. '*Foire!*' yells
she, an' wid that she grabs a bottle of greenade, an' lets
it fly. *Smash!* goes the bottle, an' doon come our twinty-
dollar ingraving av St. Patrick drivin' the shnakes out of
Ireland. *Crash!* goes another, and over comes the clock.
'Hullup!' shouts Tirry, an' got out of his chair, but *whang*,
wan of the greeners hits him in the hid an' busts all over
him. Wid that he fell spacheless on the flure, an' I thought
he wuz kilt entoirely. Tummy crawled under the sofa, an'
I scrouched doon behind the table. All this toime that
cross-eyed Mary Ann wuz screeching '*Foire! foire!*' an'
plooggin' them bottles av greenade round the room. *Bang!*
wan hits the vase full av wax fruit, that Tirry got at the
fair. *Slam!* another puts out the loight, an' clears the lamp
off the table, au' she foired the rist af the dozen bottles,
roight an' lift, *whang! smash!* round in the dark. The
glass wuz crashin', and the greenade stoof was splatterin' an'
splashin' an' tricklin' all over the wall an' furnitoor."

"Mother o' Moses!" interrupted Mr. Coogan. "It's

bushels of glass there is iverywhere. How did it ind, Mrs. Nolan ? "

" The b'yes over in the lot heard the scraychin' an' crashin', and they smothered their foire, an' come and bust in the front dure, ter see the foight they thought it wuz. Tirry is in bid, wid a poultice on his hid; an' Mary Ann is a-sittin' in the kitchen, paceable as a lamb, lookin' at the ind av her nose fer occypation. She can pack up an' lave this viry day. As fer that young sphalpeen av a Tummy, he ought ter be licked fer littin' up the winder-shade. Take my advoice, Mr. Coogan, an' trust to the foiremin or an ould-fashioned pail av water, an' don't be afther buyin' flasks av cologny-perfume to put out foires wid."

" Ye're roight, Mrs. Nolan," replied Mr. Coogan. " That's sinsible information ; an' I'll niver be google-eyed, nayther."

Life.

NINETY-EIGHT.

Who fears to speak of Ninety-Eight?
　Who blushes at the name?
When cowards mock the patriot's fate,
　Who hangs his head for shame ?
He's all a knave, or half a slave,
　Who slights his country thus ;
But a *true* man, like you, man,
　Will fill your glass with us !

We drink the memory of the brave,
　The faithful and the few :
Some lie far off beyond the wave,
　Some sleep in Ireland too ;
All, all are gone ; but still lives on
　The fame of those who died ;
All true men, like you, men,
　Remember them with pride !

Some on the shores of distant lands
　Their weary hearts have laid,
And by the stranger's heedless hands
　Their lonely graves were made ;

But though their clay be far away
　Beyond the Atlantic foam,
In true men, like you, men,
　Their spirit's still at home.

The dust of some is Irish earth;
　Among their own they rest,
And the same land that gave them birth
　Has caught them to her breast.
And we will pray that from their clay
　Full many a race may start
Of true men, like you, men,
　To act as brave a part!

They rose in dark and evil days,
　To right their native land;
They kindled here a living blaze
　That nothing shall withstand.
Alas that might should vanquish right!
　They fell and passed away;
But true men, like you, men,
　Are plenty here to-day.

Then here's their memory! may it be
　For us a guiding light,
To cheer our strife for liberty,
　And teach us to unite.
Through good and ill, be Ireland's still,
　Though sad as theirs your fate;
And true men be you, men,
　Like those of Ninety-Eight!

PAT'S BONDSMAN.

"The top av the morning to ye, Father Ray,
　Ye sees it's meself as is sober the day
　It's jist getting out of a schrape that I be,
　And Mike, that's my b'y, he went bondsman for me.

" Shure I was in court jist a fortnight ago —
　'Twas when I was over in Flannigan's Row;

And I had a fight with a neighbor or two —
They said it was murther that I was up to.

" But shure it was only a bit av a row,
And ashamed I am when I think av it now;
But one of the spalpeens fell over the stair,
And they said 'twas meself as had helped him down there.

" So they brought me in court, to his honor, Jedge Shaw,
He's a mighty hard one to come down with the law;
And the heart in my bussom could hardly kape still
When he read, ' Patrick Flynn, for attempting to kill.'

" And I trembled all over when he says to me:
' Have ye gòt any friends'll go bondsman for ye ? '
' Nary one, plaze yer honor,' sez I; then he said,
In a voice that, I reckon, would most raise the dead :

" ' Prisoner at the bar, as ye can't get no bail,
I am owthorized now to commit ye to jail.'
And then, Howly Virgin! what else should I see
But Mike walking straight to the jedge, and sez he,

" As he took off his hat, what was torn in the rim :
' Av ye plaze, Mister Jedge, *I'll* be bondsman for him.
I ain't got no money, but I'll go his bail,
And av *he* runs away you can put *me* to jail,

" ' I ain't got no mother, she died long ago,
And left me to take care of father, ye know;
And what wud she say if ye put him in jail
'Cus he hadn't got no one but me for his bail ?

" ' He's good as can be when he's not drank a drop,
And maybe if somebody asked him, he'd stop;
He didn't push Bill; I was there, and I see;
Av ye plaze, Mister Jedge, let me father go free.'

" Saints bless the child forever! The jedge sez, sez he:
' My b'y, I 'quit your father, and both av ye are free
The bail is all-sufficient; it satisfies the law.'
' Hurrah!' spoke out the people; ' three cheers for Justice
    Shaw!'

" And the jedge had some tears in his eyes, I allow,
   When he walked up to me, and sez he, with a bow:
   ' I've let ye off aisy this time, Patrick Flynn;
   For the sake av that youngster, don't come here agin.'

" So I've taken the pledge now, yer Riverence Ray,
   On account of the b'y, and I'm sober the day;
   It *was* a bad schrape, and I'd niver got free,
   Only for Mike going bondsman for me."

LILIAN A. MOULTON, *in Youth's Companion.*

WASHEE, WASHEE.

BROWN John, he bends above his tub
In cellar, alley, anywhere
Where dirt is found, why John is there;
And rub and rub and rub and rub.
The hoodlum hisses in his ear;
" Get out of 'ere, you yeller scrub!"
He is at work, he cannot hear;
He smiles that smile that knows no fear;
And rub and rub and rub and rub,
He calmly keeps on washing.

The politicians bawl and crow
To every idle chiv. and blood,
And hurl their two hands full of m
" The dirty Chinaman must go!"
But John still bends above his tub,
And rub and rub and rub and rub;
He wrestles in his snowy suds
These dirty politicians' duds;
And rub and rub and rub and rub,
He calmly keeps on washing.

" Git out o' here! ye haythin, git!
Me Frinch ancisthers fought and blid
For this same freedom, so they did,
An' I'll presarve it, ye can bit!
Phwat honest man can boss a town ?
Or burn anither Pittsburg down ?
Or beg ? Or strike ? Or labor shirk

Phile yez are here an' want to work ?
Git out, I say! ye haythin, git!"
And Silver Jimmy shied a brick
That should have made that heathen sick;
But John, he kept on washing.

Then mighty Congress shook with fear
At this queer, silent little man,
And cried, as Congress only can :
"Stop washing and get out of here!"
The small brown man, he ceased to rub,
And raised his little shaven head
Above the steaming, sudsy tub,
And unto this great Congress said,
Straightforward, business-like and true :
"Two bittee dozen washee you!"
Then calmly went on washing.

Oh! honest, faithful little John,
If you will lay aside your duds,
And take a sea of soap and suds
And wash out dirty Washington ;
If you will be the Hercules
To cleanse our stables clean of these
That all such follies fatten on,
There's fifty million souls to-day
To bid you welcome, bid you stay
And calmly keep on washing.
                              JOAQUIN MILLER.

----◆----

ANNIE'S TICKET.

PLAZE, sir, I have brought you the ticket
    You gave her a short wake ago ;
My own little girl I am manin',
    The one wid the fair hair, ye know,
And the blue eyes so gentle and tendher,
    And swate as the angels above ;
God help me, she's one of thim now, sir,
    And I've nothin' at all left to love.

It has come on me suddin, ye see, sir;
  She was niver an ailin' child,
Though her face was as white as a lily,
  And her ways just that quiet and mild.
The others was always a throuble,
  And botherin', too, ivery way,
But the first tears as iver she cost me
  Are thim that I'm sheddin' to-day.

'Twas on Tuesday night that she sickened,
  She had been as blithe as a bird
All day, wid the ticket you gave her;
  The like of it niver was heard:
"Oh, mammie, just think of the music;"
  And, "Mammie, they'll give us ice crame;
We can roll on the turf and pick posies;
  Oh, mammie, it's just like a drame!"

And so, when the fever kim on her,
  It seemed the one thought in her brain;
'Twould have melted the heart in your breast, sir,
  To hear her, again and again,
Beggin': "Mammie, oh, plaze get me ready —
  The boat will be gone off, I say;
I hear the bell ring — where's my ticket?
  Oh! won't we be happy to-day?"

Three days, sir, she raved with the fever,
  Wid her face and hands like a flame;
But on Friday, at noon, she grew quiet,
  And knew me, and called me by name.
My heart gave a lape when I heard it;
  But, oh! sir, it turned me to stone —
The look round the mouth, pinched and drawn like,
  I knew God had sent for his own.

And she knew it, too, sir, the crathur,
  And said, when I told her the day,
In her wake little voice: "Mammie darlint,
  Don't cry 'cause I'm goin' away.
To-morrow they'll go to the picnic;
  They'll have beautiful times, I know;
But heaven is like it, and betther,
  And so I am ready to go.

"And, mammie, I ain't a bit frightened,
    There's many a little girl died —
And it seems like the dear, lovin' Saviour
    Was standin' right here by my side.
Take my ticket, dear mammie, and ask
    If some other child, poor and sad,
That hasn't got heaven and Jesus,
    May go in my place and be glad."

And thin, " Wish good-by, mammie darlint,"
    She drew my lips down to her own,
Thin the One she had felt close beside her
    Bent, too, and I sat there — alone.
And so I have brought you the ticket,
    Though my heart seems ready to break,
To ask you to make some poor crathur
    Feel glad for my dear darlint's sake.

O'THELLO.

O'THELLO was a sojer bould,
    Though black he was be nature;
To Disdemony he was wed —
    An innocent young crayture.

Wid her he lived in payce an' quiet,
    For she was no vyrago,
Till on a cursed night he met
    A villin called Iago.

Sez he, " Yer wife's a perjured jade;
    Och! she's a faithless lassie — oh!
She doesn't care two pins for you,
    But she'd give her two eyes out for Casshio!

" Wid him she galivants about
    All in her hours of laysure;
To him she gave her handkerchief,
    All for to wipe his rayshure!"

Wid that he fell into a rage,
  An' riz a wondhrous riot,
An' swore he'd murdther her that night,
  Whin everything was quiet.

But not wid dagger, nor with dirk,
  For that would raise a foul sthir,
But he'd take an' blow the candle out,
  An' smother her wid the boulsther.
              HARPER'S MAGAZINE.

LANTY LEARY.

LANTY was in love, you see,
  With lovely, lively Rosie Carey,
But her father can't agree
  To give the girl to Lanty Leary.
"Up to fun, away we'll run,"
  Says she, "my father's so conthrairy,
Won't you follow me? won't you follow me?"
  "Faith, I will!" says Lanty Leary.

But her father died one day
  (I hear 'twas not from dhrinking wather);
House and land and cash, they say,
  He left by will to Rose, his daughther;
House and land and cash to seize,
  Away she cut so light and airy:
"Won't you follow me? won't you follow me?"
  "Faith, I will!" says Lanty Leary.

Rose herself was taken bad,
  The fayver worse each day was growin'.
"Lanty dear," says she, "'tis sad,
  To th' other world I'm surely goin';
You can't survive my loss, I know,
  Nor long remain in Tipperary:
Won't you follow me? won't you follow me?"
  "Faith, I won't!" says Lanty Leary.
              SAMUEL LOVER.

KATIE'S ANSWER.

Och, Katie's a rogue, it is thrue,
But her eyes, like the sky, are so blue,
    An' her dimples so swate,
    An' her ankles so nate,
She dazed, an' she bothered me, too.

Till one mornin' we wint for a ride,
Whin,' demure as a bride, by my side
    The darlint, she sat,
    Wid the wickedest hat
Neath purty girl's chin iver tied.

An' my heart, arrah, thin how it bate!
For my Kate looked so temptin' an' swate,
    Wid cheeks like the roses,
    An' all the red posies
That grow in her garden so nate.

But I sat just as mute as the dead,
Till she said wid a toss of her head,
    " If I'd known that to-day
    Ye'd have nothing to say,
I'd have gone wid my cousin, instead."

Thin I felt myself grow very bowld
For I knew she'd not scold if I towld
    Uv the love in my heart,
    That would never depart,
Though I lived to be wrinkled and old.

An' I said: " If I dared to do so,
I'd lit go uv the baste, and I'd throw
    Both arms round her waist,
    An' be stalin' a taste
Uv them lips that are coaxin' me so."

Thin she blushed a more illegent red
As she said, without raisin' her head,
    An' her eyes lookin down
    Neath her lashes so brown,
" Would ye like me to drive, Misther Ted? "

PADDY'S DREAM.

I HAVE often laughed at the way an Irish help we had at
Barnstable once fished me for a glass of whiskey. One
morning he says to me, "Oh, yer honor," says he, "I had a
great drame last night intirely ! I dramed I was in Rome,
tho' how I got there is more than I can tell : but there I was,
sure enough ; and as in duty bound, what does I do but go
and see the Pope. Well, it was a long journey, and it was
late when I got there — too late for the likes of me ; and when
I got to the palace I saw priests and bishops and cardinals,
and all the great dignitaries of the Church, a-coming out ;
and sais one of them to me, 'How are ye, Pat Moloney?'
sais he ; 'and that spalpeen yer father, bad luck to him ! how
is he ?' It startled me to hear me own name so suddent,
that it came mighty nigh waking me up, it did. Sais I,
'Your riverence, how in the world did ye know that Pat
Moloney was me name, let alone that of me father ?'—'Why,
ye blackguard !' sais he, 'I knew ye since ye was knee-high
to a goose, and I knew yer mother afore ye was born.'—
'It's good right yer honor has then to know me,' sais I. —
'Bad manners to ye !' sais he ; 'what is it ye are afther doing
here at this time o'night ?' — 'To see his Holiness, the Pope,'
sais I. 'That's right,' sais he ; 'pass on, but leave yer im-
pudence with yer hat and shoes at the door.' Well, I was
shown into a mighty fine room where his Holiness was, and
down I went on me knees. 'Rise up, Pat Moloney,' sais his
Holiness ; 'ye're a broth of a boy to come all the way from
Ireland to do yer duty to me ; and it's dutiful childen ye
are, every mother's son of ye. What will ye have to drink,
Pat ?' (The greater a man is, the more of a rael gintleman
he is, yer honor, and the more condescending.) 'What will
ye have to drink, Pat ?' sais he. 'A glass of whiskey, yer
Holiness,' sais I, 'if it's all the same to ye.'—'Shall it be
hot, or cold ?' sais he. 'Hot,' sais I, 'if it's all the same,
and gives ye no trouble.'—'Hot it shall be,' sais he ; 'but
as I have dismissed all me servants for the night, I'll just
step down below for the tay-kettle ;' and wid that he left
the room, and was gone for a long time ; and jist as he came
to the door again he knocked so loud the noise woke me up,
and, be jabers ! I missed me whiskey entirely ! Bedad, if I
had only had the sense to say 'Nate, yer Holiness,' I'd a

had me whiskey sure enough, and never known it warn't all
true, instead of a drame." I knew what he wanted, so I
poured him out a glass. "Won't it do as well now, Pat?"
said I. "Indeed it will, yer honor," says he, "and me
drame will come true, after all. I thought it would; for it
was mighty nateral at the time, all but the whiskey."

Anonymous.

LESSONS IN COOKERY.

Miss Cicely Jones is just home from boarding-school, and
engaged to be married; and, as she knows nothing about
cooking or housework, is going to take a few lessons in culi-
nary art to fit her for the new station in life which she is
expected to adorn with housewifely grace. She certainly
makes a charming picture as she stands in the kitchen-door,
draped in a chintz apron prettily trimmed with bows of ribbon, her bangs hidden under a Dolly-Varden cap, old kid
gloves, while she sways to and fro on her dainty French-kid
heels, like some graceful wind-blown flower.

"Mamma," she lisped prettily, "please introduce me to
your assistant."

Whereupon, mamma says, "Bridget, this is your young
lady, Miss Cicely, who wants to learn the name and use of
every thing in the kitchen, and how to make cocoanut rusks
and angels' food, before she goes to housekeeping for herself."

Bridget gives a snort of disfavor; but, as she looks at the
young lady, relents, and says, "I'll throy."

"And now, Bridget dear," says Miss Cicely, when they
were alone, "tell me every thing You see, I don't know any
thing, except what they did at school; and isn't this old
kitchen lovely? What makes this ceiling such a beautiful
bronze color, Bridget?"

"Shmoke," answers Bridget shortly; "and me ould eyes
are put out with that same."

"Shmoke — I must remember that; and, Bridget, what are
those shiny things on the wall?"

"Kivers? — tin kivers for pots and kittles."

"Kivers? — oh, yes; I must look for the derivation of that
word. Bridget, what are those round things in the basket?"

"Praties! (For the Lord's sake where hez ye lived niver

to hear of praties?)   Why, them's the principal mate of Ireland, where I kim from."

"Oh! but we have corrupted the name into potatoes; such a shame not to keep the idiom of a language!   Bridget — do you mind if I call you Biddie?   It is more euphonious, and modernizes the old classic appellation.   What is this liquid in the pan here?"

"Och, murder!   Where wuz ye raised?   That's millick, fresh from the cow."

"Millick?   That is the vernacular, I suppose, of milk; and that thick, yellow coating?"

"Is crame.   (Lord, such ignorance!)"

"Crame!   Now, Biddie, dear, I must get to work.   I'm going to make a cake all out of my own head for Henry — he's my lover, Biddie — to eat when he comes to-night."

Bridget [*aside*]: "It's dead he is, sure, if he ates it!"

"I've got it all down here, Biddie, on my tablet: A pound of butter, twenty eggs, two pounds of sugar, salt to your taste.   No, that's a mistake.   Oh, here it is!   Now, Biddie, the eggs first.   It says to beat them well; but won't that break the shells?"

"Well, I'd break thim this time if I were you, Miss Cicely; they might not set well on Mister Henry's stummack if ye didn't," said Bridget pleasantly.

"Oh! I suppose the shells are used separately.   There! I've broken all the eggs into the flour.   I don't think I'll use the shells, Biddie; give them to some poor people.   Now, what next?   Oh, I'm so tired!   Isn't housework dreadful hard?   But I'm glad I've learned to make cake.   Now, what shall I do next, Biddie?"

"Excuse me, Miss Cicely, but you might give it to the pigs.   It's meself can't see any other use for it," said Bridget, very crustily.

"Pigs!   O Biddie! you don't mean to say that you have some dear, cunning little white pigs!   Oh, do bring the little darlings in and let me feed them!   I'm just dying to have one for a pet!   I saw some canton-flannel ones once at a fair, and they were too awfully sweet for any thing."

Just then the bell rang, and Bridget returned to announce Mr. Henry; and Cicely told Bridget she would take another lesson the next day: and then she went up-stairs in her chintz apron and mob-cap, with a little dab of flour on her tip-lifted nose, and told Henry she was learning to cook; and he told her she must-not be overheated, or worried out, for he didn't care whether she could cook or not: he should never want to eat when he could talk to her, and it was only sordid souls that cared for cooking.

And, meanwhile, poor Bridget was just slamming things in the kitchen, and talking to herself in her own sweet idiom about "idgits turning things upside down for her inconvaniencing."   *Detroit Free Press.*

------◆------

THE IRISH TRAVELLER.

AN Irishman travelling, though not for delight,
Arrived in a city one cold winter's night;
Found the landlord and servants in bed at the inn,
While standing without, he was drenched to the skin.
He groped for the knocker, no knocker was found;
Then turning his head accidentally round,
He saw, as he thought, by the lamp's feeble ray,
The object he searched for right over the way.
The knocker he grasped, and so loud was the roar
It seemed like a sledge breaking open the door.
The street, far and wide, was awoke by the clang,
And sounded aloud with the Irishman's bang.
The wife screamed aloud, and the husband appears
At the window, his shoulders shrugged up to his ears.
"So ho, honest friend, pray what is the matter,
That at this time of night you should make such a clatter?"
"Go to bed, go to bed!" says Pat, "my dear honey,
I am not a robber to ask for your money;
I borrowed your knocker before it was day,
To waken the landlord right over the way."

------◆------

TEDDY'S SIX BULLS.

A MERRY evening party in an English country town were bantering poor Teddy O'Toole, the Irishman, about his countrymen being so famous for bulls.

" By my faith," said Teddy, "you needn't talk about that same in this place : you're as fond of bulls as any people in all the world, so you are."

" Nonsense ! " some of the party replied; " how do you make that out ? "

" Why, sure, it's very aisy, it is; for in this paltry bit of a town you've got more public houses nor I ever seen wid the sign of the bull over the doors, so you have," said Teddy.

" Nay, Teddy, very few of those ; but there's some of 'em, you know, in every town."

" Yes," said Teddy, obstinately sticking to his text, for he had laid a trap for his friends ; " but you've more nor your share, barring that you're so fond of bulls, as I say. I'm sure I can count half a dozen of 'em."

" Pooh, nonsense ! " cried the party : " that will never do. What'll you bet on that, Teddy ? You're out there, my boy, depend upon it : we know the town as well as you ; and what will you bet ? "

" Indeed, my brave boys, I'll not bet at all. I'm no better, I assure ye : I should be worse, if I wur." This sally tickled his companions, and he proceeded. " But I'll be bound to name and count the six."

" Well, do, do," said several voices.

" Now, let me see ; there's the Black Bull."

" Yes, that's one."

" Then, there's the Red Bull."

" That's two."

" And the White Bull."

" Come, that's three."

" And the Pied Bull."

" So there is ; you'll not go much farther."

" And then there's — there's — there's the Golden Bull, in — what's it street ? "

" Well done, Teddy ; there's five, sure enough ; but you're short yet."

" Ay," said the little letter-carrier, who sat smirking in the corner, " and he will be short ; for there isn't one more, I know."

" And then, remember," continued Teddy, carefully pursuing his enumeration, " there's the Dun Cow."

At this a burst of laughter fairly shook the room, and busy hands kept the tables and glasses rattling, amidst boisterous cries of, —

" A bull ! a bull ! "
Looking serious at all around, Teddy deliberately asked, —
" Do you call that a bull ? "
" ' To be sure, it's a bull," exclaimed several voices at once.
" Then," said Teddy, " that's the sixth."

A MIRACLE.

An Irish priest on miracles a sermon one day preached ;
And on his way home from the church, before his home he
   reached,
Was overtaken by a man whose name was Patrick Kent,
Who wished a miracle explained : he didn't know what one
   meant.

" A miracle, is it? " said the priest.   " You want me to explain,
So when I say a miracle, you'll know just what I mane?
Well, thin, walk on forninst me now: come, hurry and be
   quick."
The man walked on: the priest walked up, and gave Pat
   quite a kick.

" Och ! " roared the sufferer, feeling sore, " an' sure phy did
   ye that ? "
" An' did ye fale it? " asked the priest.   " Begor I did,"
   said Pat.
" Ah, ha ! ye felt it then, ye did, — ye felt the kick ye got?
Well, sir, 'twould been a miracle if ye had felt it not."

Charles H. Webber.

PAT AND MISS SKITTY.

Arrah ! you're a throublesome creathur,
   Miss Skitty, and that is quite true :
To think I should come from old Ireland,
   To be bit by a varmint like you!

Och, now, then be off with your whispers !
  Sure, you have no manners at all.
Miss Skitty, indade ! I won't *miss* ye,
  But lave ye jist flat on the wall.

Bedad, she has slipped through my fingers !
  As clean as a whistle she's gone ;
And jist as I got right forninst her,
  And wanted to pinch her back-bone !

Be aisy, now, Patrick ; keep civil :
  She's a fairy, maybe, in disguise ;
For, light as the seed of a thistle,
  Out of sight she entirely flies.

Miss Skitty, Miss Skitty, my darlint,
  Come, whisper a word in my ear.
Be aisy, now, Patrick, be aisy ;
  The bloodthirsty villain is near !

Take that, now ! Indade, I have caught her,
  And laid her out flat for her wake.
Bedad, my own cheek I've been thumping !
  Bad luck ! She has made her escape !

Faith, then, my own Skitty, my honey,
  'Tis you that are nimble of wing ;
'Tis you has the sweetest of voices ;
  Come, teach me the tunes that ye sing.

Whist ! All unbeknownst I'll steal on her ;
  She's settled hersel' on the pane.
Confess all your sins, now, Miss Skitty :
  You'll ne'er say a prayer again.

Och, now, what has happened the winder ?
  By my soul, the fairy's slipped through !
An' what shall I say to the missus ?
  For she's left a hole in it, too !

Bedad, I have cut my own knuckles !
  But sorra a bit would I care,
If only I hurted the torment
  As much as the loss of a hair.

Faith, she's an ill-mannered creathur,
  A stain on the land of the free, —
That the likes of her should be spilling
  The best blood on this side the sea!

I wisht I was back in old Ireland;
  Or else that Saint Pat lived below,
To banish the vile Miss Skitties,
  As he banished the snakes long ago.

Bessie Bently.

AT THE RISING OF THE MOON.

"Oh, then! tell me, Shawn O'Ferrall,
  Tell me why you hurry so?"
"Hush, ma bouchal, hush and listen;"
  And his cheeks were all aglow.
"I bear ordhers from the captain:
  Get you ready, quick and soon;
For the pikes must be together
  At the risin' of the moon."

"Oh, then! tell me, Shawn O'Ferrall,
  Where the gatherin' is to be?"
"In the ould spot by the river,
  Right well known to you and me.
One word more — for signal token,
  Whistle up the marchin' tune,
With your pike upon your shoulder
  By the risin' of the moon."

Out from many a mud-wall cabin,
  Eyes were watching through that night:
Many a manly chest was throbbing
  For the blessed warning light.
Murmurs passed along the valley,
  Like the banshee's lonely croon,
And a thousand blades were flashing,
  At the risin' of the moon.

There beside the singing river
  That dark mass of men was seen,
Far above the shining weapons
  Hung their own beloved green.
" Death to every foe and traitor!
  Forward, strike the marchin' tune,
And hurrah, my boys, for freedom!
  'Tis the risin' of the moon."

Well, they fought for poor old Ireland,
  And full bitter was their fate.
(Oh! what glorious pride and sorrow
  Fill the name of Ninety-eight!)
Yet, thank God, e'en still are beating
  Hearts in manhood's burning noon,
Who would follow in their footsteps
  At the risin' of the moon!

Leo Casey.

THE IRISH SCHOOLMASTER.

OLD Teddy O'Rourke kept a nice little school at a place
called Clarina, in the South of Ireland. He hadn't many
scholars, because the folks iu those parts were for the most
part too poor to send their children to school, and they
picked up their learning as pigs do their meat; still Teddy
had some pupils, though they were a roguish lot, in spite of
their having to pay a penny a week extra to be taught manners.

Teddy's schoolroom was a bit of a shed: and the boys
couldn't complain of bad ventilation, seeing that there was
a hole in the roof which left it open to the blue sky, and
the rain too; for in those parts, when the rain does pour, it
comes down mightily.

Well, one morning. says Ted, "My boys, since all of you
are here, I'll just call over your names to see that none
of you are missing. Gerald McShaa?"—"I'm here, sir."
" Paddy O'Shaughnessy?"—"Here, but my brother Barney
ain't." "Where is your brother Barney, then?"—"He's
dead, sir, and they are going to *wake* him." "Are they?
well, you go and sit down by the fire, and larn your task,
and don't be falling *asleep*, or I'll be waking *you*.—Paddy
MacShane, my darling, come here, and bring your ugly face

wid you, and spell me Constantinople."—"I can't, sir."—
"Can't you ? then by the powers I'll teach you : first of all, you
see, there's C."—"C." "O."—"O." "N."—"N." "Con."
—"Con." "That's the Con."—"That's the Con." "S."—
"S." "T."—"T." "A."—"A." "N."—"N." "Stan."
—"Stan." "That's the Stan."—"That's the Stan."
"And the Constan."—"And the Constan." "T."—"T."
"I."—"I." "Ti."—"Ti." "That's the Ti."—"That's
the Ti." "And the Stanti."—"And the Stanti." "And
the Constanti."—"And the Constanti." "N."—"N." "O."
—"O." "No."—"No." "That's the No."—"That's the
No." "And the Tino."—"And the Tino." "And the Stan-
tino."—"And the Stantino." "And the Constantino."—
"And the Constantino." "P."—"P." "L."—"L." "E."
—"E." "Ple."—"Pull." "That's the Ple."—"That's
the Pull." "And the Nople."—"And the Nopull." "And
the Tinople."—"And the Tinopull." "And the Stantino-
ple."—"And the Stantinopull." "And the Constantinople."
—"And the Constantinopull."

"Now," said Teddy to Felix O'Brian, "before you go *down,*
come *up* and say your letters. What is the name of the
first letter in the alphabet?"—"X, sir."—"No, sir. What
does your father give the donkey to eat, sir?"—"Nothing,
sir."—"And what else, sir?"—"Hay, sir."—"Aye, that's
a good boy; and what's next to A?"—"Don't know, sir."
—"What is the name of that great bird that flies about the
garden, and stings the people?"—"A wasp, sir."—"No, sir.
What is it that makes all the honey?"—"Bee, sir."—"B —
that's right; B a good boy, and mind what I say, and you'll
be a beautiful scholar. Now, the next letter to B, what is
it?"—"I don't know, sir."—"What do I do when I turn up
my eyes?"—"You squint, sir."—"And what else, sir?'—
"You see."—"C — that's right: now what's next to C?—
"W, sir."—"What is your grandmother's name?"—"Judee,
sir."—"Arrah, can't you say D without the Ju?"—"Yes,
sir, D and no Jew."—"Well, sir?"—"E, F."—"Well, what
do you stop for?"—"Because I can't go no further."—"What
do the wagoners say when they want their horses to go
faster?"—"Gee ho, dobbin."—"G, and no ho dobbin."—
"H."—"Well, that's right; and what follows H?"—"Don't
know."—"What has your mother got by the side of her
nose?"—"A pimple, sir."—"A pimple!"—"Yes, sir, and
one eye."—"I — that's a good boy: you're my head scholar,

and will soon be a man. Well, go on." — ".J." — " What's next to J?"— " I'm sure I don't know." — " What does your mother open the door with?" — " A poker, sir." — "And what besides?" — "A string, sir." — "And what else?" — "A kay, sir." — " K — that's right, to be sure, — she opens the door with a key. Now, what's next to K?"— " L."— " Well, and what's next?" — " Don't know, sir."—" What does your mother do with her nightcaps when she makes them?" — "She pawns them, sir."—"Stoopid booby! how does she make them?" — " She cuts them out, and hems them." — "Can't you say M and no cut out?" — " M and no cut out." — "I'll cut out your jacket. — What's next?" — " Don't know, sir." — " How does your mother get her eggs?"— " She buys 'em, sir." — " Doesn't the hen lay them?" — " Father sold the hen to buy whiskey." — "Och the ungrateful young scamp of an informer! take that!"—"Oh!"— " O — right at last. I thought I'd make you say O. Go on." — " I can't, sir." — " What does Biddy feed the pigs with?" — " Pays, sir, and praties."—" Say pay and no praties." — " Pay and no praties." — " And it's no praties you shall have to-day, for you'll go and stand in the corner. Send up the next boy."

HOW DENNIS TOOK THE PLEDGE.

A LIMERICK Irishman named Dennis, addicted to strong drink, was often urged by his friends to sign the pledge, but with no avail, until one day they read to him from a newspaper an account of a man who had become so thoroughly saturated with alcohol, that, on attempting to blow out a candle, his breath ignited, and he was instantly blown to atoms. Dennis's face showed mingled horror and contrition, and his friends thought that the long-desired moment of repentance was at hand.

"Bring me the book, boys, bring me the book! Troth, his breath took foir, did it? Sure, I'll niver die that death, onyhow," said Dennis, with the most solemn countenance imaginable. "Hear me now, b'ys, hear me now. I, Dennis Finnegan, knowin' my great wakeness, deeply sinsible of my past sins, an' the great danger I've been in, hereby take me solemn oath, that, so long as I live, under no provocation whativer, will I — *blow out a candil ayin!*"

WHEN McGUE PUTS THE BABY TO SLEEP.

We have a foine tinement, close be the bridge,
　　Wid three pairs of stairs and a farm.
The farm's on the roof, but it's ilegant just
　　For to kape the small childer from harm.
The railin' is high.　Shure it's tired they get
　　From playin' "puss corner" an' "peep,"
An' 'twould do your heart good in the twilight to see
　　Ould McGue put the baby to sleep.

McGue is my man, an' a daisy he is,
　　For after the gas-house shuts down
He comes wid his pail (faith, the coal on his face
　　Gives the shake to the boys of the town).
Then he sits down wid me, an' his poipe, an' his chair,
　　Comfortable, cosey, an' deep,
Wid the kid in his arms; it would break you to see
　　Ould McGue put the baby to sleep.

He sings him the chune of "The Old Phwiskey Jug,"
　　An' juggles him up on his knee
As light as the mist from ould Erin's green turf
　　That floats from the bog to the sea.
Then the gossoon lies back like a king on his couch,
　　An' the shadows across his eyes creep;
I'll lay you a bet, it's a beautiful sight,
　　When McGue puts the baby to sleep.

Then the ould man says "Phwist!" as the first darling
　　　snore
　　He hears from the swate, sleeping child;
An' he steps to the cradle, as aisy as mud,
　　An' the drop of a pin makes him wild.
"The Virgin take care of that baby!" his prayer
　　Comes out of the heart low and deep;
It would kill the ould man if the kid should refuse
　　John McGue for to put him to sleep.

THE CONFESSION.

PADDY McCABE was dying one day,
  And Father Molloy he came to confess him;
Paddy pray'd hard he would make no delay
  But forgive him his sins and make haste for to bless him.
" First tell me your sins," says Father Molloy,
" For I'm thinking you've not been a very good boy."
" Oh," says Paddy, " so late in the evenin' I fear
'Twould throuble you such a long story to hear,
For you've ten long miles o'er the mountain to go,
While the road *I've* to travel's much longer, you know:
So give us your blessin' and get in the saddle,
To tell all my sins my poor brain it would addle;
And the docthor gave ordhers to keep me so quiet —
'Twould disturb me to tell all my sins, if I'd thry it,
And your Reverence has towld us, unless we tell *all*,
'Tis worse than not makin' confession at all:
So I'll say, in a word, I'm no very good boy,
And, therefore, your blessin', sweet Father Molloy."

" Well, I'll read from a book," says Father Molloy,
  " The manifold sins that humanity's heir to;
And when you hear those that your conscience annoy,
  You'll just squeeze my hand, as acknowledging thereto."
Then the Father began the dark roll of iniquity,
And Paddy, thereat, felt his conscience grow rickety,
And he gave such a squeeze that the priest gave a roar —
" Oh, murdher!" says Paddy, " don't read any more,
For, if you keep readin', by all that is thrue,
Your Reverence's fist will be soon black and blue;
Besides, to be throubled my conscience begins,
That your Reverence should have any hand in *my* sins;
So you'd betther suppose I committed them all,
For whether they're great ones, or whether they're small,
Or if they're a dozen, or if they're four-score,
'Tis your Reverence knows how to absolve them, asthore:
So I'll say, in a word, I'm no very good boy,
And, therefore, your blessin', sweet Father Molloy,"

" Well," says Father Molloy, " if your sins I forgive,
  So you must forgive all your enemies truly;

And promise me also that, if you should live,
　You'll leave off your old tricks, and begin to live newly."
" I forgive ev'rybody," says Pat, with a groan,
" Except that big vagabone Micky Malone;
And him I will murdher if ever I can —"
" Tut, Tut!" says the priest, " you're a very bad man;
For without your forgiveness, and also repentance,
You'll ne'er go to Heaven, and that is my sentence."
" Poo!" says Paddy McCabe, " that's a very hard case,
With your Reverence and Heaven I'm content to make pace,
But with Heaven and your Reverence I wondher — *Och hone,*
You would think of comparin' that blackguard Malone —
But since I'm hard press'd and that I *must* forgive,
I forgive — if I die — but as sure as I live
That ugly blackguard I will surely desthroy! —
So, *now* for your blessin', sweet Father Molloy!"

LOVER.

FATHER PHIL'S COLLECTION.

FATHER BLAKE was more familiarly known by the name
of Father Phil. By either title, or in whatever capacity, the
worthy Father had great influence over his parish ; and there
was a free-and-easy way with him, even in doing the most
solemn duties, which agreed wonderfully with the devil-may-
care spirit of Paddy. Stiff and starched formality in any
way is repugnant to the very nature of Irishmen. There
are forms, it is true, and many, in the Romish Church ; but
they are not *cold* forms, but *attractive* rather to a sensitive
people. Besides, I believe those very forms, when observed
the least formally, are the most influential on the Irish.

With all his intrinsic worth, Father Phil was, at the same
time, a strange man in exterior manners; for, with an abun-
dance of real piety, he had an abruptness of delivery, and a
strange way of mixing up an occasional remark to his congregation in the midst of the celebration of the mass, which
might well startle a stranger. But this very want of formality made him beloved by the people, and they would do
ten times as much for Father Phil as for the severe Father
Dominick.

On the Sunday in question, Father Phil intended deliver-
ing an address to his flock from the altar, urging them to

the necessity of bestirring themselves in the repairs of the chapel, which was in a very dilapidated condition, and at one end let in the rain through its worn-out thatch. A subscription was necessary; and to raise this among a very impoverished people was no easy matter. The weather happened to be unfavorable, which was most favorable to Father Phil's purpose; for the rain dropped its arguments through the roof upon the kneeling people below, in the most convincing manner; and, as they endeavored to get out of the wet, they pressed round the altar as much as they could, for which they were reproved very smartly by his Reverence, in the very midst of the mass. These interruptions occurred sometimes in the most serious places, producing a ludicrous effect, of which the worthy Father was quite unconscious, in his great anxiety to make the people repair the chapel.

A big woman was elbowing her way towards the rails of the altar; and Father Phil, casting a sidelong glance at her, sent her to the right-about, while he interrupted his appeal to Heaven to address her thus: —

" ' *Agnus Dei* ' — You'd bether jump over the rails of the althar, I think. Go along out o' that. There's plenty o' room in the chapel below there."

Then he would turn to the altar, and proceed with the service, till, turning again to the congregation, he perceived some fresh offender.

" ' *Orate fratres!* ' — Will you mind what I say to you, and go along out o' that? There's room below there. Thrue for you, Mrs. Finn, it's a shame for him to be thramplin' on you. Go along, Darby Casy, down there, and kneel in the rain. It's a pity you haven't a decent woman's cloak under you, indeed! ' *Orate fratres!* ' "

Then would the service proceed again, till the shuffling of feet edging out of the rain would disturb him; and, casting a backward glance, he would say, —

" I hear you there! Can't you be quiet, and not be disturbin' my mass, you haythens ? "

Again he proceeded, till the crying of a child interrupted him. He looked around quickly.

" You'd bether kill the child, I think, thramplin' on him, Lavery. Go out o' that. Your conduct is scandalous. — ' *Dominus vobiscum!* ' "

Again he turned to pray; and, after some time, he made an interval in the service to address his congregation on the subject of the repairs, and produced a paper containing the names of subscribers to that pious work who had already contributed, by way of example to those who had not.

"Here it is," said Father Phil, "here it is, and no denying it, down in black and white. But if they who give are down in black, how much blacker are those who have not given at all! But I hope they will be ashamed of themselves when I howld up those to honor who have contributed to the uphowlding of the house of God. And isn't it ashamed o' yourselves you ought to be, to lave his house in such a condition? And doesn't it rain a'most every Sunday, as is he wished to remind you of your duty? Aren't you wet to the skin a'most every Sunday? Oh, God is good to you, to put you in mind of your duty, giving you such bitther cowlds that you are coughing and sneezin' every Sunday to that degree that you can't hear the blessed mass for a comfort and a benefit to you! And so you'll go on sneezin' until you put a good thatch on the place, and prevent the appearance of the evidence from Heaven against you every Sunday, which is condemning you before your faces, and behind your backs, too; for don't I see, this minute, a strame o' wather that might turn a mill, running down Micky Mackavoy's back, between the collar of his coat and his shirt?"

Here a laugh ensued at the expense of Micky Mackavoy, who certainly *was* under a very heavy drip from the imperfect roof.

"And is it laughin' you are, you haythens?" said Father Phil, reproving the merriment which he himself had purposely created *that he might reprove it.* "Laughin' is it you are at your backslidings and insensibility to the honor of God,—laughin', because when you come here to be saved, you are lost entirely with the wet? And how, I ask you, are my words of comfort to enter your hearts, when the rain is pouring down your backs at the same time? Sure, I have no chance of turning your hearts, while you are undher rain that might turn a mill. But once put a good roof on the house, and I will inundate you with piety. Maybe it's Father Dominick you would like to have coming among you, who would grind your hearts to powdher with his heavy words. [Here a low murmur of dissent ran through the throng.] Ha, ha! so you wouldn't like it, I see. Very well, very well. Take care, then; for if I find you insensible to my moderate reproofs, you hard-hearted haythens,

you malefacthors and cruel persecuthors, that won't put
your hands in your pockets because your mild and quiet
poor fool of a pasthor has no tongue in his head! I say,
your mild, quiet, poor fool of a pasthor (for I know my own
faults partly, God forgive me). And I can't spake to you
as you deserve, you hard-living vagabonds, that are as insensible to your duties as you are to the weather. I wish it
was sugar or salt that you were made of; and then the rain
might melt you, if *I* couldn't. But no. Them naked
rafthers grins in your face to no purpose. You chate the
house of God. But take care; maybe you won't chate the
Divil so aisy. [Here there was a sensation.] Ha, ha! that
makes you open your ears, does it? More shame for you.
You ought to despise that dirty enemy of man, and depend
on something better. But I see I must call you to a sense
of your situation, with the bottomless pit undher you, and
no roof over you. Oh, dear, dear, dear! I'm ashamed of
you! Throth, if I had time and sthraw enough, I'd rather
thatch the place myself, than lose my time talking to you.
Sure, the place is more like a stable than a chapel. Oh,
think of that!— the house of God to be like a stable! For
though our Redeemer was born in a stable, that is no reason
why you are to keep his house always like one.

"And now I will read you the list of subscribers; and it
will make you ashamed when you hear the names of several
good and worthy Protestants in the parish, and out of it,
too, who have given more than the Catholics."

He then proceeded to read the following list, which he
interlarded copiously with observations of his own, making
viva voce marginal notes, as it were, upon the subscribers,
which were not unfrequently answered by the persons so
noticed from the body of the chapel; and laughter was
often the consequence of these rejoinders, which Father Phil
never permitted to pass without a retort. Nor must all this
be considered in the least irreverent. A certain period is
allowed between two particular portions of the mass, when
the priest may address his congregation on any public matter, — an approaching pattern or fair or the like, in which
exhortations to propriety of conduct, or warnings against
faction, fights, etc., are his themes. Then they only listen
in reverence. But, when a subscription for such an object
as that already mentioned is under discussion, the flock con-
sider themselves entitled to "put in a word" in case of

necessity. This preliminary hint is given to the reader that he may better enter into the spirit of Father Phil's

SUBSCRIPTION LIST

FOR THE REPAIRS AND ENLARGEMENT OF BALLYSLOUGH-GUTTHERY CHAPEL.

PHILIP BLAKE, P.P.

"'Mick Hickey, £0. 7s. 6d.' He might as well have made it ten shillings. But half a loaf is betther than no bread."

"Plaze, your Reverence," says Mick, from the body of the chapel, "sure seven and sixpence is more than the half of ten shillings." (A laugh.)

"Oh, how witty you are! Faith, if you knew your prayers as well as your arithmetic, it would be betther for you, Micky."

Here the Father turned the laugh against Mick.

"'Billy Riley, £0. 3s. 4d.' Of course he means to subscribe again!

"'John Dwyer, £0. 15s. 0d.' That's something like. I'll be bound he's only keeping back the odd five shillings for a brush full o' paint for the althar. It's as black as a crow, instead o' being as a dove."

He then hurried over rapidly some small subscribers as follows : —

"'Peter Hefferman, £0. 1s. 8d.

"'James Murphy, £0. 2s. 6d.

"'Mat Donovan, £0. 1s. 3d.

"'Luke Dannely, £0. 3s. 0d.

"'Jack Quigly, £0. 2s. 1d.

"'Pat Finnegan, £0. 2s. 2d.

"'EDWARD O'CONNOR, Esq., £2. 0s. 0d.' There's for you! Edward O'Connor, Esq.,— *a Protestant in the parish,* — two pounds!"

"Long life to him!" cried a voice in the chapel.

"Amen!" said Father Phil. "I'm not ashamed to be clerk to so good a prayer.

"'Nicholas Fagan, £0. 2s. 6d.

"'Young Nicholas Fagan, £0. 5s. 0d.' Young Nick is betther than owld Nick, you see.

"'Tim Doyle, £0. 7s. 6d.

"'Owny Doyle, £1. 0s. 0d.' Well done, Owny na Coppal! You deserve to prosper, for you make good use of your thrivings.

"'Simon Leary, £0. 2s. 6d. Bridget Murphy, £0. 10s. 0d.' You ought to be ashamed o' yourself, Simon! A lone widow woman gives more than you."

Simon answered, "I have a large family, sir; and she has no childher."

"That's not her fault," said the priest. "And maybe she'll mend o' that yet." This excited much merriment; for the widow was buxom, and had recently buried an old husband, and, by all accounts, was cocking her cap at a handsome young fellow in the parish.

"'Jude Moylan, £0. 5s. 0d.' Very good, Judy. The women are behaving like gentlemen. They'll have their reward in the next world.

"'Pat Finnerty, £0. 8s. 4d.' I'm not sure if it is 8s. 4d. or 3s. 4d., for the figure is blotted; but I believe it is 8s. 4d."

"It was three and fourpince I gave, your Reverence," said Pat from the crowd.

"Well, Pat, as I said eight and fourpence, you must not let me go back o' my word: so bring me five shillings next week."

"Sure, you wouldn't have me pay for a blot, sir?"

"Yis, I would : that's the rule of backgammon, you know, Pat,—when I hit the mark, you pay for it."

Here his Reverence turned around, as if looking for some one, and called out, "Rafferty, Rafferty, Rafferty! Where are you, Rafferty?"

An old gray-headed man appeared, bearing a large plate; and Father Phil continued,—

"There, now, be active. I'm sending him among you, good people; and such as cannot give as much as you would like to be read before your neighbors, give what little you can towards the repairs; and I will continue to read out the names, by way of encouragement to you,—and the next name I see is that of Squire Egan. Long life to him!

"'Squire Egan, £5. 0s. 0d.' Squire Egan, five pounds! Listen to that! *A Protestant in the parish*, five pounds! Faith, the Protestants will make you ashamed of yourselves, if you don't take care!

"'Mrs. Flanagan, £2. 0s. 0d.'   Not her own parish, either.
A fine lady.
"'James Milligan of Roundtown, £1 0s. 0d.'   And here
I must remark that the people of Roundtown have not been
backward in coming forward on this occasion.   I have a long
list from Roundtown, — I will read it separate "   He then
proceeded at a great pace, jumbling the town and the pounds
and the people in the most extraordinary manner: "'James
Milligan of Roundtown, one pound; Darby Daly of Roundtown, one pound; Sam Finnegan of Roundtown, one pound;
James Casey of Roundpound, one town; Kit Dwyer of
Townpound, one round — pound, I mane; Pat Roundpound
— Pounden, I mane — Pat Pounden, a pound, of Pound-
town also.'   There's an example for you!
"But what are you about, Rafferty?   I don't like the
sound of that plate of yours.   You are not a good gleaner.
Go up first into the gallery there, where I see so many good-
looking bonnets.   I suppose they will give something to
keep their bonnets out of the rain; for the wet will be into
the gallery next Sunday, if they don't.   I think that is
Kitty Crow I see, getting her bit of silver ready.   Them
ribbons of yours cost a thrifle, Kitty. — Well, good Chris-
tians, here is more of the subscription for you : —
"'Matthew Lavery, £0 2s. 6d.'   *He* doesn't belong to
Roundtown.   Roundtown will be renowned in future ages
for the support of the Church.   Mark my words, Roundtown will prosper from this day out; Roundtown will be a
rising place.
"'Mark Hennessy, £0 2s. 6d.; Luke Clancy, £0. 2s. 6d.;
John Doolin, £0. 2s. 6d.'   One would think they had all
agreed only to give two and sixpence apiece; and they comfortable men, too!   And look at their names, — Matthew,
Mark, Luke, and John, — the names of the blessed Evan-
gelists; and only ten shillings among them!   Oh, they are
apostles not worthy the name!   We'll call them the poor
apostles from this out.   [Here a low laugh ran through the
chapel.]   Do you hear that, Matthew, Mark, Luke, and
John?   Faith, I can tell you that name will stick to you."
(Here the laugh was louder.)
A voice, when the laugh subsided, exclaimed, "I'll make
it ten shillin's, your Reverence."
"Who's that?" said Father Phil.
"Hennessy, your Reverence."

"Very well, Mark. I suppose Matthew, Luke, and John will follow your example."

"We will, your Reverence."

"Ha! I thought you made a mistake. We'll call you now the faithful apostles, and I think the change in your name is better than seven and sixpence apiece to you.

"I see you in the gallery there, Rafferty. What do you pass that well-dressed woman for? Thry back. Ila! see that. She had her money ready, if you only asked her for it. Don't go by that other woman there. Oh, ho! So you won't give any thing, ma'am! You ought to be ashamed of yourself. There is a woman with an elegant sthraw bonnet, and she won't give a farthing. Well now, afther that, remember — I give it from the althar — that, from this day out, sthraw bonnets pay fi'penny pieces.

"'Thomas Durfy, Esq., £1. 0s. 0d.' It's not his parish, and he's a brave gentleman.

"'Miss Fanny Dawson, £1. 0s. 0d.' *A Protestant out of the parish*, and a sweet young lady, God bless her! Oh, faith, the Protestants is shaming you!

"'Dennis Fannin, £0. 7s. 6d.' Very good indeed for a working mason.

"'Jemmy Riley, £0. ⤬ 5s. 0d.' Not bad for a hedge carpenther."

"I gave you ten, plaze, your Reverence," shouted Jemmy. "And by the same token, you may remember it was on the Nativity of the blessed Vargin, sir, I gave you the second five shillin's."

"So you did, Jemmy," cried Father Phil. "I put a little cross before it, to remind me of it. But I was in a hurry to make a sick-call when you gave it to me, and forgot it afther. And, indeed, myself doesn't know what I did with that same five shillings."

Here a pallid woman, who was kneeling near the rails of the altar, uttered an impassioned blessing, and exclaimed, "Oh, that was the very five shillings, I'm sure, you gave to me that very day, to buy some little comforts for my poor husband, who was dying in the fever!" And the poor woman burst into loud sobs as she spoke.

A deep thrill of emotion ran through the flock as this accidental proof of their poor pastor's beneficence burst upon them. And as an affectionate murmur began to rise above the silence which that emotion produced, the burly

Father Philip blushed like a girl at this publication of his charity, and, even at the foot of that altar where he stood, felt something like shame in being discovered in the commission of that virtue so highly commended by the Providence to whose worship that altar was raised. He uttered a hasty "Whisht, whisht!" and waved with his outstretched hands his flock into silence.

In an instant one of those sudden changes so common to an Irish assembly, and scarcely credible to a stranger, took place. The multitude was hushed, the grotesque of the subscription-list had passed away and was forgotten, and that same man and that same multitude stood in altered relations, — *they* were again a reverent flock, and *he* once more a solemn pastor. The natural play of his nation's mirthful sarcasm was absorbed in a moment in the sacredness of his office; and, with a solemnity befitting the highest occasion, he placed his hands together before his breast, and, raising his eyes to heaven, he poured forth his sweet voice, with a tone of the deepest devotion, in that reverential call for prayer, "*Orate fratres!*"

The sound of a multitude gently kneeling down followed, like the soft breaking of a quiet sea on a sandy beach. And when Father Philip turned to the altar to pray, his pent-up feelings found vent in tears, and while he prayed he wept.

I believe such scenes as this are of not unfrequent occurrence in Ireland, — that country so long-suffering, so much maligned, and so little understood.

O rulers of Ireland! why have you not sooner learned to *lead* that people by love, whom all your severity has been unable to *drive?*

Samuel Lover.

ST. PATRICK'S MARTYRS.

I wonder what the mischief was in her! for the mistress was niver contrairy;
But this same is just what she said to me, just as sure as my name is Mary:
"Mary," says she, all a-smiling and swate like, "the young ladies are coming from France,
And we'll give them a welcome next Monday, with an elegant supper and dance."

" Is it Monday, ye're maning ? " says I, " ma'am ; why, thin,
  I'm sorry to stand in yer way,
But it's little of work I'll do Monday, seeing that Monday's
  St. Patrick's Day ;
And sure it's meself that promised to go wid Cousin Kitty
  Malone's brother Dan,
And bad luck to Mary Magee," says I, "if she disappoints
  such a swate young man ! "

" Me children have been away four years," — and she spoke
  in a very unfeelin' way, —
" Ye cannot expect I shall disappoint them either for you or
  St. Patrick's Day :
I know nothing about St. Patrick." — " That's true for ye,
  ma'am, more's the pity," says I,
" For it's niver the likes of ye has the luck to be born under
  the Irish sky."

Ye see I was getting past jokin' — and she sitting there so
  aisy and proud,
And me thinking of the Third Avenue, and the procession
  and music and crowd ;
And it crossed me mind that minit consarning Thady Mulligan's supper and dance.
Says I, " It's not Mary Magee, ma'am, that can stay for ladies
  coming from France."

" Mary," says she, " "two afternoons each week — ivery
  Wednesday and ivery Monday —
Ye've always had, besides ivery early Mass, and yer Vespers
  ivery other Sunday ;
And yer friends hev visited at me house, two or three of
  them ivery night."
" Indade thin," says I, " that was nothin' at all, but ivery
  dacent girl's right ! "

" Very well, thin," says she, " ye can lave the house, and be
  sure to take wid ye yer ' right ; '
And if Michael and Norah think just as ye do, ye can all of
  ye lave to-night."
So just for St. Patrick's glory we wint ; and, as sure as Mary
  Magee is me name,
It's a house full of nagurs she's got now, which the same is
  a sin and a shame.

Bad luck to them all! A body, I think, had need of a comfortable glass;

It's a miserable time in Ameriky for a dacent Irish-born lass.

If she sarves the saints, and is kind to her friends, then she loses her home and her pay,

And there's thousands of innocent martyrs like me on ivery St. Patrick's Day.

PAT'S CORRESPONDENCE.

WHIST now! till I relate to you my — well, yer what now? Oh! I hev it, me — no I heven't it thin. What is it? It's letter-writing any how — now what do ye call it? Ah! ha! now I hev it — *correspondence*, that's the wourd.

You know I wrote a letter to Tim Flanagin: Tim wrote a letter to me. Tim lives in the ould country: I live in the new. That's the difference between Tim and me. The *difference* did I say? Well, now! that wourd makes me think of something I can't but tell till ye. It was the other day whin I was walking up Broad Street, I heard some one a-calling out "Pat!" seys he. "What do ye want?" sed I. "I want till talk to ye," sed he. "Well, talk away, thin," sed I. "Come along here, why don't ye thin?" — "Where air ye that I may come?" But jist thin I see a big red-nosed fellow peaking from behint a lamp-post. "Well, now," sed I to meself, "I don't know who thet fellow is at all at all. I'll go over any how and see what he wants o' the likes of me." So over I wint, and as I got within speaking distance he seys to me, seys he, "How air ye, Pat?" — "What's thet to a mon I don't know?" sed I. "Oh, well, Pat, me boy," sed he, "niver mind thet; I hev a skanumdrum for ye." "A *what?*" said I. "A skanumdrum," sed he; "I'm going to ask" — "Ask nothing," sed I; "but give me thet — what do ye call it? — the first thing ye do." — "Yer not understanding me," sed he; "I mean by thet a riddle." — "Oh, ho! a riddle is it? Out wid it thin; for it's many a wone I guessed in the ould country." — "Thin guess me this. What is the difference between yourself and a pig?" — "Air ye joking?" sed I. "Not a bit of it, Pat; can ye tell?" Well jist thin one of the durty bastes passed us wid his — [*grunt-*

ing like a pig]. " Hear thet," sed I ; "it's not in the voice
any how." After scratching me head a while, I sed to him,
" I'll give it up." — " Why, Pat, me boy, there is no difference
at all." — " Ain't there ! Look-a-here, young man, thet may
be what ye call a skanumdrum in Ameriky, but I give ye to
understand thet in the ould country it would be a signal for
the sudden dislocation of yer big red nose, and so it would."
He didn't stop to hear it all, and it was well for him, or me
name's not Pat.

After looking at him a while, I turned once more on me
way, end I hed not gone far before I heard another cry of
" Pat ! " — " Oh, ho ! sed I to meself, " here is another one of
thim skanumdrum, I suppose. Who air ye ? where air ye ?
and what do ye want ? " sed I, all in a breath. " I'm here,
and it is a-speaking to ye I want," sed a green-looking fellow over the way. " Well," sed I to meself, " I'll go over
and see what the blackguard wants wid me." So over I
wint, and the very first thing was, " Pat, I hev a skanumdrum
for ye." — " I thought so," sed I to meself ; thin sed to him,
" Well, what is it thin ? " — " Tell me, Pat, the difference
between yourself and a pig." — " Me boy, that is ould," sed
I in a whisper ; thin I sed to him, " Repeat it." He did.
" Look me in the eye," sed I. " I'm looking," sed he. " Now,
ye want to know the difference between me and a pig ? "
" That's it," sed he. I looked at *him*, thin at *meself*, thin at
him agin ; thin I walked over to him, thin back agin, pacing
it off so — [*walking four or five paces*]. Thin looking right at
him, I sed, " Do ye moind, I'm not good at guessing, but
after pacing it, I would say *the difference between me and a
pig is about six feet.*" Well, if ever a mon looked beat he
did ; and wid a good — [*slapping his sides and crowing*] I left
him.

But my dear friends what hes all this to do wid me correspondence ? " Nothing," seys you. Well, thin, to go back to
it. Tim wrote, seys he, " Pat, your own living uncle is now
dead ; and all he had is to be given to you and me, his only
heirs, saving fourteen others. Come thin, Pat, and git your
share." Well, I jist set down and wrote, " Tim, yer a fool.
Don't bother yer head wid a few paltry pounds, but come at
once to the best country in the wourld. Why, Tim, there is
no hanging for stealing here ! Pertaties are only twenty-five
cents a bushel, wid whiskey the same ! And more than thet,
Tim, ye git yer three dollars a day for doing nothing at all ;

for all ye have to do is to make a three-cornered box, fill it
wid bricks, carry it up a three-story building, and *you will
find a mon there, wid a trowel, thet will do all the wourk.*"

W. M. GIFFIN.

LITTLE PAT AND THE PARSON.

HE stands at the door of the church, peeping in,
    No troublesome beadle is near him ;
The preacher is talking of sinners and sin,
    And little Pat trembles to hear him.

A poor little fellow, alone and forlorn,
    Who never knew parent or duty ;
His head is uncovered, his jacket is torn,
    And hunger has withered his beauty.

The white-headed gentleman shut in the box,
    Seems growing more angry each minute ;
He doubles his fist, and the cushion he knocks,
    As if anxious to know what is in it.

He scolds at the people who sit in the pews, —
    Pat takes them for kings and princesses.
(With his little bare feet, he delights in their shoes ;
    In his rags, he feels proud of their dresses !)

The parson exhorts them to think of their need,
    To turn from the world's dissipation,
The naked to clothe, and the hungry to feed, —
    Pat listens with strong approbation !

And when the old clergyman walks down the aisle,
    Pat runs up to meet him right gladly,
" Shure, give me my dinner ! " says he, with a smile,
    " And a jacket, — I want them quite badly."

The kings and the princesses indignantly stare,
    The beadle gets word of the danger,
And, shaking his silver-tipped stick in the air,
    Looks knives at the poor little stranger.

But Pat's not afraid, he is sparkling with joy,
  And cries, — who so willing to cry it?
"You'll give me my dinner, — I'm such a poor boy:
  You said so, — now don't you deny it."

The pompous old beadle may grumble and glare,
  And growl about robbers and arson;
But the boy who has faith in the sermon stands there,
  And smiles at the white-headed parson!

The kings and princesses may wonder and frown,
  And whisper " He wants better teaching;"
But the white-headed parson looks tenderly down
  On the boy who has faith in his preaching.

He takes him away without question or blame,
  As eager as Patsy to press on,
For he thinks a good dinner (and Pat thinks the same)
  Is the moral that lies in the lesson.

And after long years, when Pat, handsomely drest, —
  A smart footman, — is asked to determine
Of all earthly things what's the thing he likes best.
  He says, " Och, shure, the master's ould sermin!"

PATRICK O'ROUKE AND THE FROGS.

A COLD WATER STORY.

St. Patrick did a vast deal of good in his day: he not
only drove the snakes out of Ireland, but he also drove
away the frogs, — at least I judge so from the fact that
Patrick O'Rouke was unfamiliar with the voices of these
noisy hydropaths. Pat had been visiting at the house of a
friend, and he had, unfortunately, imbibed more whiskey than
ordinary mortals can absorb with safety to their persons.
On his return home the road was too narrow, and he per-
formed wonderful feats in his endeavors to maintain the
centre of gravity. Now he seemed to exert his best efforts
to walk on both sides of the road at the same time; then he
would fall and feel upward for the ground; then he would

slowly pick himself up, and the ground would rise and hit him square in the face. By the time he reached the meadow-lands, located about half-way betwixt his home and the shanty of his friend, he was somewhat sobered by the ups and downs he had experienced on the way.

Hearing strange voices, he stopped suddenly to ascertain, if possible, the purport of their language. Judge his aston-ishment when he heard his own name distinctly called, "Pat-rick O'Rouke! Patrick O'Rouke!"

"Faith, that's my name, sure."

"Patrick O'Rouke! Patrick — O'Rouke — Rouke — Rouke!"

"What do ye want o' the likes o' me?" he inquired.

"When did you come over — come over — come over?"

"It is jest tree months ago to the minute, and a bad time we had, sure, for we wur all say-sick, and the passage lasted six long wakes."

"What will you do — do — do? What will you do — do — do?"

"I have nothing to do at all at all; but then I can do any thing: I can dig; I can tind mason; and I can hould office — if I can git it."

"You are drunk — you are drunk — drunk — drunk — drunk — drunk!"

"By my sowl, that's a lie!"

"You are drunk — dead drunk — drunk — drunk!"

"Repate that same if ye dare, and I will take me shillaly to ye!"

"You are drunk — dead drunk — drunk — drunk!"

"Jist come out here now and stip on the tail o' my coat, like a man!" exclaimed Pat, in high dudgeon, pulling off his coat and trailing it upon the ground.

"Strike him — strike him — strike — strike — strike!"

"Come on wid ye, and the divil take the hindmost; I am a broth of a boy — come on!"

"Knock him down — down — down!"

"I will take any one in the crowd; and if Mike Mulligan was here we wud take all of yees at onct."

"Kill him — kill him — kill him!"

"Och, murther! sure ye wud not be after murdering me — I was not oncivil to ye. Go back to Pate Dogan's wid me now, and I will trate ivery one of yees."

"We don't drink rum — rum — rum."

" And are ye all Father Mathew men ? "

"We are cold-water men — water men."

" Take me advice now, and put a little whasky in the wather, darlings : it will kape the cowld out whin yees git wet, and so it will."

" Moderation — moderation — moderation."

"Yis, that's the talk. I wint to Pate Dogan's, down there in Brownville, and says I, ' Will ye stand trate ? ' Says he, ' Faith, and I will.' Says I, ' Fill up the glass ; ' and so he did. ' Fill it agin,' said I, and so he did; ' and agin,' said I, and so he did. ' Give me the bottle,' said I. ' And I won't do that same,' said he. ' Give me the bottle,' said I, and he kipt on niver heedin' me at all at all, so I struck him wid me fist rite in his partatee thrap, and he kicked me out o' the house, and I took the hint that he didn't want me there, so I lift."

" Blackguard and bully — blackguard and bully."

" Ye wouldn't dare say that to my face in broad day, sure ; but ye are a set of futpads and highwaymin, hiding behind the rocks and the traas. Win I onct git to Watertown I will sind Father Fairbanks afther ye, and he will chuck ye into the pond as he did that thafe who stole the public money, and he will hould ye there until ye confess, or he will take yees to the perleese."

" Come on, boys — chase him — chase him ! "

· " Faith, and I won't run, but I will jist walk rite along, for if any of me frinds shud find me here in sich company, at this time o' night, they wud think I was thrying for to stale somethin'. Tak me advice, boys, and go home, for it's goin' for to rain, and ye will git wet to the skin if ye kape sich late hours."

" Catch him — catch him — catch him ! "

" Sure, ye'd bether not, for I haven't got a cint wid me, or I'd lave it in yer jackets. What's the use of staling all a man has whin he has jist nothing at all at all ? Bad luck to ye for bothering me so."

About this time the frog concert was in full tune, and the hoarse chorus so alarmed Pat that he took to his heels, for he was now sober enough to run. Reaching his home, two miles distant from the scene of his encounter with the " highwaymin " who held such a long parley with him, he gave a graphic history of his grievance. Soon it was noised about the neighborhood that Patrick O'Rouke had been waylaid and abused by a drunken set of vagabonds, whose headquarters were near a meadow on the banks of the Black River; but the fear of the citizens subsided when they discovered that Pat had been out on a bender, and could not distinguish a frog from a friend or an enemy.

GEORGE W. BUNGAY.

WIDOW MALONE.

DID you hear of the Widow Malone,
Ohone !
Who lived in the town of Athlone,
Alone !
Oh, she melted the hearts
Of the swains in them parts :
So lovely the Widow Malone,
Ohone !
So lovely the Widow Malone.

Of lovers she had a full score,
Or more ;
And fortunes they all had galore,
In store.
From minister down
To the clerk of the Crown,
All were courting the Widow Malone,
Ohone !
All were courting the Widow Malone.

But so modest was Mistress Malone,
'Twas known
That no one could see her alone,
Ohone !
Let them ogle and sigh,
They could ne'er catch her eye,
So bashful the Widow Malone,
Ohone !
So bashful the Widow Malone.

Till one Misther O'Brien, from Clare,
(How quare!
It's little for blushing they care
Down there)
Put his arm round her waist,
Gave ten kisses at laste,
"Oh," says he, " you're my Molly Malone,
My own!
Oh," says he, " you're my Molly Malone!"

And the widow they all thought so shy,
My eye!
Ne'er thought of a simper or sigh, —
For why?
But, " Lucius," says she,
" Since you've now made so free,
You may marry your Mary Malone,
Ohone!
You may mary your Mary Malone."

There's a moral contained in my song,
Not wrong;
And one comfort, it's not very long,
But strong, —
If for widows you die,
Learn to kiss, not to sigh;
For they're all like sweet Mistress Malone,
Ohone!
Oh, they're all like sweet Mistress Malone!

Charles Lever.

THE BIRTH OF ST. PATRICK.

On the eighth day of March it was, some people say,
That Saint Pathrick at midnight he first saw the day;
While others declare 'twas the ninth he was born,
And 'twas all a mistake between midnight and morn, —
For mistakes *will* occur in a hurry and shock, —
And some blamed the babby, and some blamed the clock;
Till with all their cross-questions sure no one could know
If the child was too fast, or the clock was too slow.
Now the first faction fight in owld Ireland, they say,
Was all on account of Saint Pathrick's birthday!

Some fought for the eighth — for the ninth more would die;
And who wouldn't see right, sure they blackened his eye!
At last both the factions so positive grew,
That *each* kept a birthday; so Pat then had *two*,
Till Father Mulcahy, who showed them their sins,
Said "No one could have two birthdays, but a *twins*."
Says he, "Boys, don't be fightin' for eight or for nine,
Don't be always dividin', but sometimes combine.
Combine eight with nine, and seventeen is the mark,
So let that be his birthday." — "Amen," says the clerk,
"If he wasn't a *twins*, sure our hist'ry will show
That, at least, he's worth any *two* saints that we know!"
Then they all got blind dhrunk — which complated their
 bliss,
And we kept up the practice from that day to this.

SAMUEL LOVER.

MURPHY'S MYSTERY OF THE PORK-BARREL.

"MURPHY, what's the meaning of mystery? Faith, I was reading the paper, and it said 'twas a mystery how it was done."

"Well," said Murphy, "Pat, I'll tache ye. Ye see, when I lived with my father, a little gossoon, they gave me a parthy; and me mother wint to market to buy somethin' for the parthy to ate, and among the lot of things, she bot a half-barrel of pork, ye see. Well, she put it down in the cellar, bless her sowl, for safe keeping, till the parthy come on, do ye see. Well, when the parthy come on, me mother sint me down to the cellar to get some of the pork, do ye see. Well, I wint down to the barrel and opened it, and fished about, but not a bit of pork could I find; so I looked around the barrel to see where the pork was, and found a rat-hole in the bottom of the barrel, where the pork had all run out and left the brine standing, do ye see."

"Hould on, Murphy, wait a bit! Now tell me how could all the pork get out ov the barrel, and lave the brine standing?"

"Well, Pat," said Murphy, "that's what I'd like to know myself, do you see: there's the mystery."

ANON.

PADDY BLAKE'S ECHO.

ONE OF THE WONDERS OF KILLARNEY.

In the gap of Dunlo
There's an echo, or so,
And some of them echoes is very surprisin';
You'll think, in a stave
That I mane to desaive,
For a ballad's a thing you expect to find lies in.
But visibly thrue
In that hill forninst you
There's an echo as plain and safe as the banks, too;
But civilly spake,
"How d'ye do, Paddy Blake?"
The echo politely says, "Very well, thank you!"

One day Teddy Keogh
With Kate Connor did go
To hear from the echo such wondherful talk, sir;
But the echo, they say,
Was conthrairy that day,
Or perhaps Paddy Blake had gone for a walk, sir.
So Ted says to Kate,
"'Tis too hard to be bate
By that deaf and dumb baste of an echo, so lazy;
But if we both shout
At each other, no doubt
We'll make up an echo between us, my daisy!

Now, Kitty," says Teddy,
"To answer be ready."
"Oh, very well, thank you!" cried out Kitty, then, sir.
"Would *you* like to wed,
Kitty darlin'?" says Ted.
"Oh, very well, thank you!" says Kitty, again, sir.
"D'ye like *me?*" says Teddy;
And Kitty, quite ready,
Cried, "Very well, thank you!" with laughter beguiling.
Now won't you confess
Teddy could not do less
Than pay his respects to the lips that were smiling?

Oh, dear Paddy Blake,
May you never forsake
Those hills that return us such echoes endearing!
And, girls, all translate
The sweet echoes like Kate,
No faithfulness doubting, no treachery fearing.
And, boys, be you ready,
Like frolicsome Teddy.
Be *earnest* in loving, though given to *joking;*
And thus when inclined,
May all true lovers find
Sweet echoes to answer from hearts they're invoking!

SAMUEL LOVER.

A COOK OF THE PERIOD.

THE looks of yer, ma'am, rather suits me;
The wages ye offer 'ill do;
But thin I can't inter yer sarvice
Without a condition or two.
And now, to begin, is the kitchen
Commodgeous, with plenty of light,
And fit, ye know, fur intertainin'
Sech fri'nds as I'm like to invite?

And nixt, are yous reg'lar at male-times?
Becase, 'taint convainyent, ye see,
To wait, and if I behaves punkshul,
It's no more than yous ought to be.
And thin is your gurrels good-natured?
The rayson I lift my last place,
The French nuss was sich a high lady,
I sint a dish-cloth at her face.

And have yer the laste of objiction
To min droppin' in whin they choose?
I'v got some enlivinin' fust cousins
That frayquintly brings me the news.
I must have thim trayted powlitely;
I give yer fair warnin', ma'am, now,
If the airy gate be closed agin thim,
You'll find me commincin' a row.

These matthers agrayed on between us,
 I'd try yer a wake, so I wud
(She looks like the kind I can manage,
 A thin thing without any blud!)
But mind, if I comes for a wake, ma'am,
 I comes for that time, and no liss ;
And so, thin, purvidin' ye'd want me,
 Jusht give me yer name and addriss.

LARRY'S ON THE FORCE.

WELL, Katie, and is this yersilf?   And where was you this
  whoile?
And ain't ye dhrissed?   You are the wan to illusthrate the
  stoile !
But never moind thim matthers now — there's toime enough
  for thim ;
And Larry — that's me b'y — I want to shpake to you av
  him.

Sure, Larry bates thim all for luck ! — 'tis he will make his
  way,
And be the proide and honnur to the sod beyant the say —
We'll soon be able — whist ! I do be singin' till I'm hoorse,
For iver since a month or more, my Larry's on the foorce !

There's not a proivate gintleman that boords in all the row
Who houlds himsilf loike Larry does, or makes as foine a
  show :
Thim eyes av his, the way they shoine — his coat and but-
  thons too —
He bates thim kerrige-dhroivers that be on the avenue !

He shtips that proud and shtately-loike, you'd think he
  owned the town ;
And houlds his shtick convanient to be tappin' some wan
  down.
Aich blissed day I watch to see him comin' up the shtrate,
For, by the greatest bit av luck, our house is on his bate.

The little b'ys is feared av him, for Larry's moighty shtrict,
And many's the litthle blagyard he's arristed, I expict;
The beggyars gets acrass the shtrate — you ought to see
   thim fly —
And organ-groindhers scatthers whin they see him comin' by.

I know that Larry's bound to roise; he'll get a sergeant's
   post,
And afther that a captaincy widhin a year at most;
And av he goes in politics he has the head to throive —
I'll be an Aldherwoman, Kate, afore I'm thirty-foive!

What's that again? Y'are jokin', surely — Katie! — *is* it
   thrue?
Last noight, you say, *he* — *married?* and Aileen O'Donahue?
O, Larry! c'u'd ye have the hairt — but let the spalpeen be:
Av he demanes himsilf to *her*, he's nothing more to me.

The ugly shcamp! I always said, just as I'm tellin' you,
That Larry was the biggest fool av all I iver knew;
And many a toime I've tould mesilf — *you* see it now, av
   coorse —
He'd niver come to anny good av he got on the foorce!

IRWIN RUSSELL.

PAT AND THE FROGS.

[Imitate.]

THE spring had come
With its gentle rain;
And the frogs, from
Their beds of mud,
Waked up again;
Tuned up their pipes
Of various tones,
From the shrill piccolos
To the sturdy trombones.
They were chanting in concert,
With strains of great glee,
When Pat came along
On a pretty big spree.

No money had he
The "craythur" to buy,
And oh, he was feeling
So terribly dry!
So the only chance left
For a drink, that he found,
Was the water that flowed
In the jolly frog's pond.
He came to the brink
With a "skip and a leap,"
When a tempting small voice
Cried, "knee deep! knee deep!"
"Thank you kindly," said Pat,
"Ye're right well behavin';
So I'll take aff me brogues,
An' me feet I'll be lavin'."
So he took off his boots,
Threw them down on the ground,
When a sepulchral tone
Said, "You'll dr-r-r-*rown!* You'll dr-r-r-*rown!*"
"Howly Biddy!" said he,
"It's me narves ye'd by thryin'!
Ye're a murderin' set
Of t-hieves at lyin'!
Me name's Paddy Flinn,
O' the county o' Claff-yeur!
So kom out ivery wan
An' I'll tak the scalp aff yer!
If there's iver a wan of yees
Has any spunk!" —
But the answer he got
Was: "You're dr-r-r-*runk!* dr-r-r-*runk! unk!*"
"Drunk, am I? Faith
An' it's my way of t'inkin'
If I'd live as yees do,
I'd always be drinkin'!
Not wa-ther but whiskey
I'd live in, be-gum! —
Will yees howld yer hush, iver?"—
"More r-r-r-*rum!* More r-r-r-*rum!*"
Pat picked up a stone,
Which he threw with his might,
And the voices at once
Were silenced outright.

So he put on his brogues,
On his way cogitating,
Their want of politeness
And manners berating.
Said he, " I'll go bail that
There'd be no more bother,
If whiskey they lived in,
Instid of cowld wa-ther ! "

R. M. T.

PADDY'S COURTING.

BIDDY MACHREE was a gentlewoman, — at least, as gentle
a woman as could be found anywhere. Biddy was young
and decidedly good-looking. Biddy had a neat little cot-
tage, with a good-sized potato-patch, and some fine pigs in
the sty. No wonder, then, that all the young sparks in the
neighborhood fell in love with, and fell out about, her.

Amongst the young fellows who stood a good chance of
winning the love and potato-patch of Biddy, was young
Patrick O'Conner.

He was a smart, handsome young fellow, with bright, rov-
ing eyes, and a saucy expression about the mouth that won
the good-will of everybody. His patch of land joined Biddy's,
his pigs grunted in chorus to Biddy's, the smoke of his chim-
ney always went in the direction of Biddy's, — when the wind
blew that way, — and so he began to think he had a right to
Biddy.

As to Biddy herself, she often looked in the direction of
Paddy's plot, and sighed to think of the waste of ground on
which the low stone wall stood.

One night she was sitting all alone knitting stockings, when
all of a sudden the latch was lifted, and Paddy O'Conner
entered.

" Och, murther ! " exclaimed the frightened damsel, " wher
did ye spring from ? "

" From jest nowhere, me darlint," replied Pat, who was
glad to find the charmer alone, — " from jest nowhere. I
come to spake till ye on vary partic'lar bizness."

" The ould 'ooman's fast asleep, so ye may jest spake what
ye plaze."

" Och, thin, Biddy ! " said Paddy, drawing his stool close to hers, and putting his arm round her waist, — "Och, thin, it's yerself as I've come to spake about, an' nothin' else at all, at all."

"Ye can't say much about me, for sure."

"Whew, Biddy darlint! I drame of ye."

"Och, Pat, you wouldn't be afther tellin' me your drames, would yer?"

"What if I did, me jewel? Drames come true sometimes. Be jabers, an' don't I wish my drame would come true!"

"Do yer?" said Biddy, drawing her three-legged stool nearer to his. "Tell me what it was about, honey."

"Oh, it was jest about yeself, me darlint! I dreamt I was going to church" —

"Yes, Pat."

"Yes, I dreamt I was going to church to be" —

"Christened, Pat?"

"Divil a bit was it christened; no, no, I was going to church to be" —

"Buried?"

"Buried, i' faith! not buried at all, at all. I dreamt I was going to church to be married."

"Married! O Patrick! it was only a drame, wasn't it?"

"Bad luck to it, yes; it was only a drame."

"O Paddy! will it ever come true?"

"Sure, and I'm draming it will."

"An' who was the misthress, Pat?"

"Who? Be all that's wonderful, can't yer guess?"

"Norah McCarty?"

"Why, she squints!"

"Madge Mulligan?"

"The timper of a she-wolf. No, me jewel, it was yerself."

"O Pat!" exclaimed the damsel, hiding her face in her apron, — "O Pat! I'm surprised at yer drame; for sure it was a strange drame."

They sat in silence for some moments; and Paddy, after waiting for her to uncover her face, ventured to pull down one corner of her apron and take a peep. The roguish twinkle in her eye encouraged him; so, summoning up all his fortitude, he said, —

"Will the drame come true, darlint?"

The maiden's cheek flushed a deeper crimson, and, laying her hand on his arm, she replied, "Wheniver ye plaze, Pat."

W. A. EATON.

A BIT OF GOSSIP.

I'VE just come from Mrs. Brady's,
  Who urged me to stay to tea,
" For I've got a wonderful story
  You really must hear," says she.
And with that the strings of my bunnit
  I soon began to untie.
" I'm glad you came in to-day," says she.
  " But I mustn't stay late," says I.

" You remember Mary McGinnis,
  And the airs she put on," says she;
"For the matter of that, no lady
  More stuck up with pride could be;
And I thought she would come to sorrow,
  With holding her head so high,
And not a cent in her pocket," says she.
  " To be sure she would," says I.

" They came from Ballysloughgannon,"
  Says Mrs. Brady, says she;
" And it ain't for the likes of them to look
  With scorn on the likes o' me;
For them that has lain on feathers
  May be glad on straw to lie,
And luck don't last in this world," says she.
  " Indeed an' it don't," says I.

" There's Terence," says Mrs. Brady,
  As she stirred her cup of tea,
" There isn't a better-looking boy,
  Or a dacenter one," says she;
"And that he loved Mary McGinnis
  I'm not the one to deny.
She was none too good for him," says she.
  " Of course she wasn't," says I.

" It took me so of a sudden,"
  Says Mrs. Brady, says she;
" I couldn't think it was true at all,
  But Mrs. O'Shaughnessy

Had seen it herself in the papers,
　So you know it could be no lie;
And Mary McGinnis — oh, don't she strut! "
　" More shame to her then," says I.

" An' must you go, Mrs. Doolan? "
　Says Mrs. Brady to me,
As I drew my chair from the table,
　After drinking six cups of tea.
" I haven't told you the story,"
　Says she ; " now do sit by,
For I know you're dying to hear it."
　" But it's getting late," says I.

" And," says I, " the rest of the story
　It isn't worth while to repeat,
And I wonder Mary McGinnis
　Can show her face in the street.
And," says I, " it is well that Terence
　Conducted himself so shy ;
He might have had to share the disgrace
　Of the shameless hussy,' says I.

" What's that? " says she in a minute,
　Says Mrs. Brady, says she.
" The wicked thing that you're hinting at
　Is wonderful news to me."
Says I, " You told it to me yourself."
　" I didn't," says she in reply.
" Well, you'd better tell it over again,"
　Says I, " Mrs. Brady," says I.

" So I will," says she in a hurry,
　" For I see it is getting late.
I told you Mary McGinnis
　Had heired such a big estate,
That none in Ballysloughgannon
　Could carry their heads so high,
And Terence is broken-hearted."
　" I shouldn't wonder," says I.
　　　　　　　JOSEPHINE POLLARD.

PADDY AND HIS PIG.

In the town of Kilkenny lived Paddy O'Rann,
A broth of a boy, though a true Irishman :
He could reap, he could dig, o'er the boys he could plod,
He could shoulder a musket, as well as a hod ;
In faith, there was nothing but what Pat could do ;
Both his work and his wages he could always get thro'.
Pat's father, when living, was gentle and kind ;
And when dying, he left Pat a fortune behind, —
A hay-rake, a sickle, a hoe, and two spades,
Some forks without handles, some knives without blades,
A pig in the sty, and of platters a set,
Besides all the money that Paddy could get,
With this piece of advice, to be inwardly taken,
That while he kept the pig, Pat would then save his bacon ;
But if trouble came on him, whether little or big,
Never to part with the favorite pig.
Pat kept these last words as true as a law, —
The pig lived in the cabin, and slept on clean straw :
He'd ne'er part with the pig while to keep it was able.
The grunter fed with him, underneath the same table ;
They shared both alike, through thicks and through thins,
Pat ate all the potatoes, the pig had the skins ;
They never had words, botheration, or strife,
Soon as part with his pig he would part with his life.
To save up his money, from his father he learnt it,
Spending every rap before ever he earned it ;
That brought poverty on him, — life's cruel curse.
So he kept on improving, by still getting worse.
Still, on keeping the pig, Pat Rann's mind was bent,
Till the landlord kept bothering him for the rent,
Saying, " Paddy O'Rann, now do as you please,
If you don't pay your rent, to-morrow I'll seize."
What was to be done ?   Faith ! Pat could not tell ;
Much against his consent, sure, the pig he must sell.
His father's words smote him, — he grieved at the thing ;
But he soon had the pig-hog's leg in a string.
The hog proved pig-headed and mighty ill-bred ;
For, faith, she would neither be driven nor led :
She kicked up such pranks that she'd not done before,
And Pat found that his *sow* was a terrible *boar* (bore).

She first went at a gallop, then she was slow,
Every step she took forwards, she backwards did go ;
She would then give a jump, a grunt, and a squall,
Capsized an old woman and her apple-stall.
" Arrah ! you're off, thin, to market," Mike Fagan did say.
" Hush !" cried Pat, " if she hears you, she'll not go that
      way."
Just as if she had heard every word that did drop,
She set off at a gallop that Pat could not stop ;
And, to add to poor Paddy's pleasures and joys,
They were hooted and pelted by a whole troop of boys.
" Och ! she's going down the wrong street, now. Och ! "
     cried Pat, " I'm no dunce.
She'll go up all manner of streets, faith, at once."
                      ANONYMOUS.

TEDDY McGUIRE AND PADDY O'FLYNN.

TEDDY TO PADDY.

    OCH, Paddy O'Flynn !
    Are yez at it agin ?
Drink-drinking away wid the lame and the lazy?
    Sure, it's small wit yez had,
    At yer soberest, lad ;
So what can it be whin yer head has gone crazy
    Wid whiskey and gin ?
    Foolish Paddy O'Flynn !

    Och, Paddy O'Flynn,
    See the pickle yer in !
Bare elbows and toes, dhirt and raggedness, Paddy.
    Saint Patrick would shame
    To be spakin' yer name ;
Wouldn't own yez a son of ould Ireland, me laddy.
    But the divils would grin
    To see Paddy O'Flynn !

    Och. Paddy O'Flynn,
    While yer spendin' for gin,
Or whiskey, gossoon, what yer nadin' for dinner,

Yer mither half dead
For praties and bread,
Sits cryin' her eyes out, ye graceless young sinner!
Not worth a bent pin,
Drunken Paddy O'Flynn!

Och, Paddy O'Flynn,
Sich a wurrld as we're in!
Topsy-turvey wid sorrow, how can yez be makin'
More trouble and care,
More grafe and despair,
More wapin' and wailin' and bitter heart-brakin',
More vileness and sin,
Wicked Paddy O'Flynn?

Och, Paddy O'Flynn!
Aich tumbler of gin
Is an ocean too dape for a sowl, — it betrays ye.
Whin once yez go down,
Ye're certain to drown.
If yez float, the say-sarpent is likely to saze ye;
And where are yez thin,
Wretched Paddy O'Flynn?

Och, Paddy O'Flynn!
Stand up, and begin
To look like a crature half-dacent and human!
Fath! I'll give yez me hand
Wid a bit of me land;
And I'll lind yez a shpade, and I'll kape the ould woman
Till yer crops ye get in,
Neighbor Paddy O'Flynn!

Och, Paddy O'Flynn!
There's a heaven to win.
Hooray! smash the glass! shpill the shtuff, so defilin'!
How the divils will howl
Whin they see yer poor sowl
Makin' tracks up the sky wid the angels all smilin'
To welcome yez in,
Happy Paddy O'Flynn!

PADDY TO TEDDY.

Och, Teddy McGuire!
Me heart's batin' higher
To be gratin' yez here on American sile.
'Tis tin years, be dad,
Since I saw yez, me lad,
On that sorrowful day whin I left the Grane Isle.
A friend ye had been
To poor Paddy O'Flynn:
Ye had loved him, and lifted him out of the mire;
And me mither died blessin' yez, Teddy McGuire.

Och, Teddy McGuire!
I can spake like the squire;
But the ould tongue is best, when I mate an ould friend.
Here's a watch in me vest,
Like a birrd in its nest, —
I've praties in plenty, and money to spend.
Come home wid me, thin,
And see Mistress O'Flynn;
And she'll trate yez to somethin' ye're sure to desire:
It's a bountiful counthry, dear Teddy McGuire.

Och, Teddy McGuire!
No nade to inquire
If I've been at the whiskey-jug.   Here is my hand,
As dacent and clane
As the hand of a quane,
And sthrong at the grip.   Not a man in the land
Could brag of more muscle,
Or bate in a tussle
Wid Paddy O'Flynn; and, troth, ye'll admire
The good clothes I'm wearin' now, Teddy McGuire!

Och, Teddy McGuire!
If ye sthay in the fire,
There's no help at all, but ye're sure to be roastin'.
Lord love yez to-day
That yez dragged me away,
And chated the divil in spite of his boastin'.
Let him rage if he plaze;
I'll not barter me aise,
Nor burn up me soul for the thavish ould liar:
I've done wid the whiskey-shops, Teddy McGuire.

Look, Teddy McGuire !
There's a church wid a shpire,
And beyant, a white house wid a terrace below;
Bay-windows complate, —
Now, isn't it nate ?
Wid roses all round it beginnin' to blow;
Wid a lawn in the sun
Where the childer can run,
An orchard behind it, a barn, and a byre, —
And that is me residence, Teddy McGuire !

Och, Teddy McGuire,
Make haste and come nigher !
There's me wife in the portico watching for me.
A swate Yankee girl,
Wid a heart like a pearl,
And a will of her own, as ye're likely to see.
Her father was mad
Whin I courted her, lad :
He'd give her no money, he swore in his ire ;
But she loved me, and married me, Teddy McGuire.

Thin, Teddy McGuire,
I was workin' for hire,
Wid a beautiful farm and a dairy to tend ;
But the ould man relinted,
And left us, contided,
A snug little fortune to kape us, me friend.
See the childer come out
Wid a rush and a shout, —
The swate little cratures ! — to welcome their sire
Wid laughter and kisses, dear Teddy McGuire.

Och, Teddy McGuire !
Me blood is on fire,
Me heart it is batin' like waves of the say.
So great is me bliss
To be spakin' like this,
And bringin' yez home to me darlin's this day,
Sure, I think whin yez die,
All the angels will cry, —
" Here's the man that saved Paddy O'Flynn mountin' higher !
Make room for the swate soul of Teddy McGuire."

AMANDA T. JONES.

PAUDEEN O'RAFFERTY'S SAY-VOYAGE.

SURE now, ladies and gintlemen, if ye plase, I'll relate the great mistake I made when I came hare to Naples — stop ! aisy, Paudeen, and don't decaive the ladies and gintlemen; for, bedad ! I didn't come at all, — they brought me in a ship, a grate big ship, with two big sticks standing out of it. Masts they call thim, bad luck to it and the day I saw it ! If I had been an ignorant fellow, and didn't know joggraphy and the likes, I'd be safe enough at home now, so I would, in my own cellar on the Coal-Quay in Dublin. But I must be making a man of myself, showing my learnin', me knowl-edge of similitude and the likes. You see, I wint over to England on a bit of an agricultural speculation — hay-makin' and harvist-rapin' — and, the saison bein' good, I realized a fortune, so I did, — a matter of thirty shillings or so.

So, says I to myself, says I, " Now I have got an indipin-dent competence, I'll go back to Ireland: I'll buy it out, and make meself imperor of it." So I axed one of the boys which was my nearest way to Bristol to go be the say. So, says one of thim (be the same token he was a cousin of mine — one Terry O'Rafferty — as dacint a boy as you could wish to meet, and as handy with a shillaly. Why, I've seen him clear a tint at Donnybrook fair in less than two minutes, with nivir a won to help except his bit of a stick; and you know that's no aisy job).

" Well," says Terry to me, says he, " go down to the quay," says he, " and you'll find out all about it while a cat'd be lickin' her ear."

Well, I wint to a man that was standin' be the dure of a public-house. It was the sign of — the sign — What the plague is this the sign was? — you see, I like to be sarcum-spectius in me joggraphy. It was the sign of the blind cow kicking the dead man's eyes out, or the dead man's cow kick-ing the blind — no — well, it was something that way, any-how.

So says I to the man, " Sir," says I, " I want a ship."

" There you are," says he.

" Where ? " says I.

" There," says he.

" Thank you," says I. " Which of thim's for Ireland ? "

" Oh ! you're an ould countryman," says he.

" How did you find that out ? " says I.

" I know it," says he.

" Who tould you? " says I.

" No matther," says he.　" Come," says he.

"I will," says I.

Well, we wint in and we had half a pint of whiskey.　Oh, bedad ! it'd have done your heart good to see the bade rise on the top of it.　Maybe my heart didn't warm to him, and his to me — ow, murther !

" Erin go bragh !" says he.

" Ceadh mille failthe !" says I.

And there we wor like two sons of an Irish king in less than a minute.

Thin we got to discoorsing about Dublin and Naples, and other furrin parts that we wor acquainted with; and he began talking about how like the Bay of Naples was to the Bay of Dublin, — for, you see, he was an ould soger, d'ye mind? an' thim old sogers are always mighty 'cute chaps. He was a grate big chap that was off in the wars among the Frinch and Spaniards and the Rushers and other barbarians. So we got talking of similitude an' joggraphy an' the likes, an' mixin' Naples an' wather and Dublin an' whiskey ; and, be me sowl, purty punch we made of it.

I was in the middle o' me glory, whin in walks the captain o' the ship.

" Any one here to go aboord ? " says he.

" Here I am," says I.

And be the same token, me head was quite soft with the whiskey, and talkin' about Dublin an' Naples, an' Naples an' whiskey, and wather an' Dublin, Dublin an' Naples, Naples an' Dublin, — bad 'cess to me ! but I said the one place instead of the other when they axed me where I was going, d'ye mind ?

Well, they brought me aboord the ship as dhrunk as a lord, and threw me down in the cellar, — the hould, they called it; and the divil's own hould it was, — wid sacks, pigs, praties, an' other passengers, an' there they left me in lavendher, like Paddy Ward's pig.

I fell asleep the first week.　Whin I woke up didn't I heave ahead in me sthomatics enough to make me backbone and me ribs strike fire ?

" Arrah !" says I to meself, says I, " are they ever going to take me home ? "

Just thin I h'ard a voice sing out, —
" There's the bay."
That was enough for me. I scrambled up-stairs till I got
on the roof — the deck, they call it — as fast as my legs
could carry me.
" Land ho! " says one of the chaps.
" Where? " says I.
" There it is," says he.
" For the love of glory, show me where," says I.
" There, over the cat's-head," says he.
I looked around, but the niver the cat's head or dog's tail
aither I could see. The blaggard stared at me as if I was a
banshee or a fairy. I gev another look, and there was the
bay, sure enough, afore me.
" Arrah, good luck to you! " said I, "but you warm the
cockles of me heart. But what's come over the Hill of
Howth ? " says I. " It used to be a civil, paiceable soort of
a mountain, but now it's splutthering an' smokin' away like
a grate big lime-kiln. Sure the boys must have lit a big
bone-fire on top of it to welcome me."
With that, a vagabone that was listenin' to me cries out,
in a horse-laugh, —
" Hill of Howth! " says he. " You're a Grecian — that's
not the Hill of Howth."
" Not the Hill of Howth? " says I.
" No," says he; "that's Mount Vesuvius."
" Aisy, aisy," says I. "Isn't Mount Vesulpherous in
Italy ? "
" Yis," says he.
" An' isn't Italy in France? " says I.
" Of coorse," says he.
" An' isn't France in Gibberalther? " says I.
" To be sure," says he.
" An' isn't Gibberalther in Russia? " says I.
" Maybe so," says he, "but we're in Italy, anyhow. This
is the Bay of Naples, and that is Mount Vesuvius."
" Are you sure? " says I.
" I am," says he.
And, be me sowl, it was thrue for him. *The ship made a
big blundher* in takin' me to Naples whin I wanted to go to
Dublin, d'ye mind.

IRISH ASTRONOMY.

A veritable myth, touching the constellation of O'RYAN, ignorantly and falsely spelled ORION.

O'RYAN was a man of might
    Whin Ireland was a nation ;
But poachin' was his heart's delight,
    And constant occupation.
He had an ould militia gun,
    And sartin sure his aim was :
He gave the keepers many a run,
    And wouldn't mind the game laws.

St. Pathrick wanst was passin' by
    O'Ryan's little houldin',
And as the saint felt wake and dhry,
    He thought he'd enther bould in.
"O'Ryan," says the saint, "avick !
    To praich at Thurles I'm goin' ;
So let me have a rasher, quick,
    And a dhrop of Innishowen."

" No rasher will I cook for you
    While betther is to spare, sir;
But here's a jug of mountain dew,
    And there's a rattlin' hare, sir."
St. Pathrick he looked mighty sweet,
    And says he, " Good luck attind you !
And when you're in your windin'-sheet,
    It's up to heaven I'll sind you."

O'Ryan gave his pipe a whiff —
    " Them tidin's is thransportin',
But may I ax your saintship if
    There's any kind of sportin' ? "
St. Pathrick said, " A Lion's there,
    Two Bears, a Bull, and Cancer " —
" Bedad," says Mick, " the huntin's rare !
    St. Pathrick, I'm your man, sir !"

So, to conclude my song aright,
  For fear I'd tire your patience,
You'll see O'Ryan any night
  Amid the constellations.
And Venus follows in his track,
  Till Mars grows jealous raally;
But, faith, he fears the Irish knack
  Of handling his shillaly.

CHARLES G. HALPINE.

PADDY McGRATH'S INTRODUCTION TO MR. BRUIN.

An Irish Story.

NOT long since, 1 was walkin' with Jimmy Butler through a thick wood on me way to Judy O'Flinn's, to pay me bist addrissis to her, whin Jimmy very suddintly cried out, " Be jabers! but there's Mr. Bruin!" and with that he runs off like a shot, lavin' me alone jist forninst the ould gintleman.

"Mr. Bruin, are ye?" says I. "How do you do, Mr. Bruin? Happy to know yer worship, and hope yer honor's well. Happy o' yer acquaintance," says I. A grunt was the only answer I resaved.

"Och, sure!" thinks I, "yer a quare ould chap at iny rate;" and thin I axed him how Mrs. Bruin and all the young spalpeen Bruins prospered. He only gev me another grunt. "Bad luck to yer eddication!" says I. "Where did ye hev yer bringin' up? Me name's Paddy McGrath, of Tipperary County, ould Ireland; at yer sarvice," says I agin, thinkin' to hev some conversation wid him. He only showed me his big grinders, and gev me another grunt, but he still stood lookin' at me. "Bedad! but he's niver been taught his letthers, and cannot understhand me, or his eyes must be mighty wake and bad. The top o' the mornin' to yez! Do yez always wear yer coat with the wool on the outside?" says I agin.

This samed to touch a tinder pint wid him, and he kem towards me. Holdin' out me hand, I wint to mate him.

" Excuse the complimint," says I, "but you've a mighty oogly moog, so ye hev."

He grinned mighty plazed like, and held out his arrums to embrace me. Jist as I kem widin rache of his long arrums, he gev me a cuff aside me hid, which sint me flyin'. Me sinsis lift me mighty quick afther he sthruck me; and whin they kem back, I found mesel' a-rollin' down a shtape hill, wid no chance to sthop. Prisintly, howiver, I sthruck a big stoomp, and suddintly shtopped. Whin I got on me fate agin, I saw Mr. Bruin comin' afther me on his hands and knase, and grinnin' as much as to say, "I beg yer pardin, but I didn't mane to tip yez so hard."

" Och, I furgive yez," says I : "come to me arrums, Mr. Bruin. Paddy McGrath is not the filler to hould a groodge agin a frind. Yer as welcome to me embrace as me own Judy." This samed to plaze the ould gint mightily, for he shtood on his fate, and agin held out his arrums: I rushed to his embrace widout another word.

" Och, murdher ! murdher !" I scramed; " yer a practised hugger, ye are ! ye've been in the business afore ! How I pity Mrs. Bruin if ye sarve her this way often ! Och, murdher !" I cried agin; " I don't like such tight squazin' I'll be satisfied wid the little ye've gev me if ye'll loosen yer hould, and gev me a rist."

He gev me a harder squaze than iver, and opened his big, oogly jaws, and tried to bite me nose off.

" Bedad! are ye a haythen cannibal," says I, "that ye'd take a filler's hid off to show yer love for him?"

He gev me another hug, and fastened his big taath onto me lift shoulder. " Bad cess to ye !" says I, "but yer afther makin' too fra wid me on short acquaintince ; but I'll be aven wid yez;" so sayin', I twisted me arrum from his grasp, and, thrustin' me shillaly into his mouth, gev it a twist with such mighty force that I broke his under jaw.

The ould gint samed to think he had been too lovin' wid me; so givin' a grunt, he let go me shoulder, takin' a pound of me tinder flish wid him, which he ate with a big relish.

" Bedad, Paddy! if yez don't outdo yer new friend, he'll lave but little of yez for yer Judy," thinks I; and widout more ado I gev him a blow between his eyes. He gev a quick jerk back, and I sprang from his embrace — but, och! deary me! he took the whole of me fine coat, weskit, and shirt but the shlaves, and started off wid 'em. " Och! ye

thavin', murdherin' nager," says I, "bring back me close, or
I can't pay me addrissis to me Judy darlint."

He niver paid me a bit o' notice, but rooshed off. I
shtarted afther the haythenish baste.

He climbed up a big tra mighty quick, takin' me close
wid him. I axed him, very perlite like, to throw down me
wearin' apparel; but he only blinked his bloody eyes at me.

I was jist goin' to throw me shillaly at him, when I heard
a gun go off; and Mr. Bruin gev a terrible squail, dhropped
me close, and kem toomblin' to the ground. I looked
around in astonishment, and saw Jimmy Butler and siveral
others comin' down the hill towards me.

Whin Jimmy saw me alive, he cried like a spalpeen, and
rushed into me arrums. When he let me go, I axed him
what he mint by shootin' Mr. Bruin in that way. He told
me he was a bear and would hev kilt me. "A bear! did
ye say?" says I: "why didn't yez tell me afore, so that I
could hev kipt ye company in yer runnin' away from him?
A bear!" says I agin, beginnin' to trimble for fear the ould
gint might not be quite dead: "give him another shot,
Jimmy, to be sure ye've kilt him intirely."

He was dead sure enough, and we lift him alone quite
gory.

Jimmy got me some new close, and we wint home.

Whin I told Judy of the squazin' I got, she blushed, and
put her arrums around me nick, and gev me so soft a squaze,
that for a time I forgot me introduction to Mr. Bruin.

LARRIE O'DEE.

Now, the Widow McGee
And Larrie O'Dee
Had two little cottages out on the green,
With just enough room for two pig-pens between.
The widow was young, and the widow was fair,
With the brightest of eyes, and the brownest of hair:
And it frequently chanced, when she came in the morn
With the swill for her pig, Larrie came with the corn;
And some of the ears that he tossed from his hand,
In the pen of the widow were certain to land.

One morning said he,
" Och ! Misthress McGee,
It's a waste of good lumber, this runnin' two rigs,
Wid a fancy partition between our two pigs ! "
" Indade, sure it is ! " answered Widow McGee,
With the sweetest of smiles upon Larrie O'Dee.
" And thin it looks kind o' hard-hearted and mane
   Kapin' two frindly pigs so exsadingly near
   That whinever one grunts, thin the other can hear,
And yit keep a croel partition betwane."

" Shwate Widow McGee ! "
Answered Larrie O'Dee,
" If ye fale in your heart we are mane to the pigs,
Ain't we mane to ourselves to be running two rigs ?
Och ! It made my heart ache when I paped through the
   cracks
Of me shanty, lasht March, at yez shwingin' yer axe,
An' a-bobbin' yer head, an' a-shtompin' yer fate,
Wid yer purty white hands jusht as red as a bate,
A-sphlittin' yer kindlin'-wood out in the shtorm,
Whin one little shtove it would kape us both warm ! "

" Now, piggy," said she,
" Larrie's courtin' me,
Wid his delicate, tinder allusions to you ;
So now yez musht tell me jusht what I must do.
For, if I'm to say yes, shtir the shwill wid yer shnout,
But if I'm to say no, yez musht kape yer nose out.
Now, Larrie, for shame ! to be bribin' a pig
By a-tossin' a handful of corn in its shwig ! "
" Me darling, the piggy says yes," answered he ;
And that was the courtship of Larrie O'Dee.

                        W. W. FINK.

IRISH COQUETRY.

SAYS Patrick to Biddy, " Good-mornin', me dear !
It's a bit av a sacrit I've got for yer ear :
It's yoursel' that is lukin' so charmin' the day,
That the heart in me breast is fast slippin' away."
" 'Tis you that kin flatther," Miss Biddy replies,
And throws him a glance from her merry blue eyes.

"Arrah, thin," cries Patrick, "'tis thinkin' av you
That's makin' me heart-sick, me darlint, that's thrue!
Shure I've waited a long while to tell ye this same,
And Biddy Maloney will be such a foine name!"
Cries Biddy, "Have done wid yer talkin', I pray;
Shure me heart's not me own for this many a day!

"I gave it away to a good-lookin' boy,
Who thinks there is no one like Biddy Malloy;
So don't bother me, Pat; jist be aisy," says she.
"Indade, if ye'll let me, I will that!" says he.
It's a bit of a flirt that ye are, on the sly:
I'll not trouble ye more, but I'll bid ye good-by."

"Arrah, Patrick!" cries Biddy, "an' where are ye goin'?
Shure it isn't the best of good manners ye're showin'
To lave me so suddint!" — "Och, Biddy," says Pat,
"You have knocked the cock-feathers jist out av me hat."
"Come back, Pat!" says she. "What fur, thin?" says he.
"Bekase I meant you all the time, sir!" says she.

MEDLEY DIALECT RECITATIONS.

Edited by GEORGE M. BAKER.

BOARDS 50 CENTS . . . . *PAPER 30 CENTS.*

LEE & SHEPARD, Publishers, Boston.

CONTENTS.

		PAGE
Hans Breitmann's Party . . .	*Charles G. Leland*	5
The Deutsch Maud Muller . .	*Carl Pretzel*	6
The Dutchman's Serenade . .	. . . .	7
Dyin' Vords of Isaac	*Anon.*	9
Lookout Mountain, 1863 — Beutelsbach, 1880	*George L. Catlin*	10
Der Shoemaker's Poy	. . . .	12
Der Drummer	*Charles F. Adams*	13
The Yankee and the Dutchman's Dog	. . . .	14
Setting a Hen	. . . .	16
"What's the Matter with that Nose?"	*Our Fat Contributor* . . .	17
Keepin' the De'il oot	*Mrs. Findley Braden* . . .	19
The Puzzled Census-Taker . .	*John G. Saxe*	22
Dutch Security	. . . .	23
The Frenchman and the Rats .	. . . .	24
Heinz von Stein	*Charles G. Leland, from the German*	26
The Solemn Book-Agent . . .	*Detroit Free Press*	27
The Mother-in-Law	*Charles Follen Adams* . .	28
Schneider's Tomatoes	*Charles F. Adams*	29
Dutch Humor	. . . .	30
Squire Houston's Marriage Ceremony	. . . .	31
Dot Delephone	. . . .	31
The United Order of Half-Shells	. . . .	33
Why no Scotchmen go to Heaven	. . . .	35
Yawcob Strauss	*C. F. Adams*	36
Leedle Yawcob Strauss — what he says	*Arthur Dakin*	37
Isaac Rosenthal on the Chinese Question	*Scribner's Monthly* . . .	38
"Der Dog und der Lobster" . .	*Saul Sertrew*	39
"Der Wreck of der Hezberus".	. . . .	41
Signs and Omens	. . . .	43
A Dutchman's Answer	. . . .	44
The Vay Rube Hoffenstein sells	. . . .	45
A Dutch Recruiting Officer . .	. . . .	46
Dot Baby off Mine	. . . .	47
Dot Leetle Tog under der Vagou	. . . .	49
Schnitzerl's Velocipede . . .	*Hans Breitmann*	50
The Latest Barbarie Frietchie .	. . . .	51

PAGE

Mr. Hoffenstein's Bugle		52
Fritz and his Betsy fall out	*George M. Warren.*	54
Cut, Cut Behind	*Charles Follen Adams*	57
Tickled all Oafer		58
An Error o' Judgment		59
Sockery Kadahcut's Kat		61
I vash so Glad I vash Here!		63
Dot Shly Leedle Raskel		64
A Jew's Trouble	*Harwood*	65
Der Mule shtood on der Steam-		
boad Deck	*Anon.*	66
Teaching him the Business		67
Der Good-lookin Shnow		69
How Jake Schneider went Blind		71
The Dutchman and the Raven		72
The Dutchman who gave Mrs.		
Scudder the Small-Pox		74
Ellen McJones Aberdeen	*W. S. Gilbert*	76
A Dutch Sermon		78
Shacob's Lament		79
Mr. Schmidt's Mistake	*Charles F. Adams.*	81
John and Tibbie Davison's Dis-		
pute	*Robert Leighton*	82
Fritz und I	*Charles F. Adams*	84
A Tussle with Immigrants	*Philip Douglass.*	86
A Doketor's Drubbles	*George M. Warren*	86
Charlie Machree	*William J. Hoppin.*	90
A Dutchman's Dolly Varden	*Anon.*	91
The Frenchmen and the Flea-		
Powder		92
The Frenchman and the Sheep's		
Trotters		94
I rant to Fly		96
The Frenchman's Mistake		98
"Two Tollar?"	*Detroit Free Press.*	100
A Frenchman on Macbeth	*Anon.*	101
Like Mother used to Make	*James Whitcomb Riley, in New-York Mercury.*	101
John Chinaman's Protest		102
The Whistler		104
Mother's Doughnuts	*Charles Follen Adams*	105
Over the Left	*W. C. Dornin*	106
A Jolly Fat Friar		107
The Enoch of Calaveras	*F. Bret Harte*	107
Curly-Head	*B. S. Brooks.*	109
Warning to Woman		111
An Exciting Contest		112
A Laughing Philosopher		114
In der Shweed Long Ago	*Oofty Gooft*	117
Dot Stupporn Pony	*Harry Woodson.*	118
Spoopendyke opening Oysters	*Stanley Huntley*	119
To a Friend studying German	*Charles Godfrey Leland.*	122
Tammy's Prize		124
The Scotchman at the Play		128
An Irish Love-Letter	*Geo. M. Baker*	133

NEGRO DIALECT RECITATIONS.

Edited by GEORGE M. BAKER.

BOARDS 50 CENTS . . . . *PAPER 30 CENTS.*

LEE & SHEPARD, Publishers, Boston.

CONTENTS.

		PAGE
De 'Sperience of de Reb'rend Quako Strong		5
Tobe's Monument	*Elizabeth Kilham* . .	7
Greatest Walk on Record.		14
The New Dixie		15
A Short Sermon		16
The "Ole Marster's" Christmas . .	*Atlanta Constitution* .	18
A Sermon for the Sisters	*Irwin Russell* . . .	19
The Learned Negro		20
Art Matters in Indiana		21
Virginny	*S. N. Cook*	24
Uncle Reuben's Baptism		26
How Persimmons Took Car' ob der Baby	*Lizzie W. Champney* .	29
"Business" in Mississippi		33
The Flood and the Ark		34
Brudder Johnson on "'Lectricity"		38
Reviving de Sinners.		39
Daddy Worthless	*Lizzie W. Champney* .	41
Uncle Remus' Revival Hymn		43
A New Version of the Parable of the Virgins		44
Uncle Mellick Dines with His Master		45
No Color Line in Heaven		47
Goin' to Eliza's	*T. N. Cook*	48
Counting Eggs	*Texas Siftings* . . .	49
The Housetop Saint	*Mrs. J. D. Chaplin* .	51
Casabianca (Colored)		56
A Modern Sermon		57
Plantation Proverbs.	*J. Russell Fisher* . .	60
A Colored Debating Society		61
The Wonderful Tar-baby Story . .	*Harris*	63
Blind Ned	*Irwin Russell* . . .	64
On the Shores of Tennessee . . .	*E. L. Beers*	66
Suckers on de Corn		69
A Colored Sermon		70
A Blessing on the Dance		73
Brer Rabbit and the Butter . . .	*Harris*	74

		PAGE
"Treadwater Jim"	"*Old Si*"	77
My Little Ned is Dead	*Modern Argo*	79
The Ship of Faith		80
The Mississippi Miracle	*Irwin Russell*	81
De Pint wid Ole Pete		83
He wasn't Ready		84
Kyarlina Jim		85
Old Daddy Turner		86
The Lime-Kiln Club	*M. Quad*	88
Nebuchadnezzar		91
Dem Codicils		92
Uncle Ned's Defence		93
Sambo's Dilemma		94
The First Banjo		95
Brother Gardner on Liars		97
The Cotton-field Hand		98
Old Sambo Puzzled		99
Uncle Pete and Marse George		100
Petah		103
Meriky's Conversion		104
Chicken on the Brain		107
"Whar's de Kerridge?"		108
Go-Morrow, or Lot's Wife		111
Darkey's Counsel to the Newly Married	*Edmund Kirke*	113
Bashful		114
Brother Anderson's Sermon	*Thomas K. Beecher*	115
Uncle Dan'l's Prayer	*Mark Twain*	118
The Darkey Bootblack		121
Miss M'lindy's Courtship	*Detroit Free Press*	124
George Washington		126
A Fruitful Discourse		127

THE READING CLUB AND HANDY SPEAKER. Being Selections in Prose and Poetry, Serious, Humorous, Pathetic, Patriotic, and Dramatic, for Readings and Recitations. Edited by GEORGE M. BAKER. Paper cover, fifteen cents each part.

CONTENTS OF READING-CLUB NO. 1.

At the Soldiers' Graves.
Battle-Hymn.
"Boofer Lady," The.
Bricklayers, The.
Bumpkin's Courtship, The.
Charles Sumner.
"Curfew must not ring To-night."
Closet Scene, The. ("Hamlet.")
Defiance of Harold the Dauntless.
Der Drummer.
Deutsch Maud Muller, The.
Doorstep, The.
Factory-girl's Diary, The.
Farmer Bent's Sheep-washing.
Godiva.
"Good and Better."
Happiest Couple, The. (From the "School for Scandal.")
Happy Life, The.
Hans Breitmann's Party.
Hour of Prayer, The.
How Terry saved his Bacon.
How He saved St. Michael's.
In the Tunnel.
Jakie on Watermelon-pickle.
Jester's Sermon, The.
"Jones."

Mahmoud.
Mistletoe-Bough, The.
Mr. Caudle and his Second Wife.
Mr. O'Gallagher's Three Roads to Learning.
Nobody There.
Old Age.
Old Farmer Gray gets Photographed.
Old Methodist's Testimony, The.
Overthrow of Belshazzar.
Puzzled Census-Taker, The.
Popping the Question.
Red Jacket, The.
Rob Roy MacGregor.
Samson.
Senator's Pledge, The.
Showman's Courtship, The.
Squire's Story, The.
Story of the Bad Little Boy who didn't come to Grief, The.
Story of the Faithful Soul, The.
Stranger in the pew, A.
Tauler.
Voices at the Throne, The.
Whistler, The.
Yankee and the Dutchman's Dog, The.

CONTENTS OF READING-CLUB NO. 2.

Address of Spottycus.
Baby Atlas.
Baby's Soliloquy, A.
Beauty of Youth, The.
Biddy's Troubles.
Bobolink, The.
Broken Pitcher, The.
By the Alma River.
Calling a Boy in the Morning.
Cooking and Courting.
Curing a Cold.
Double Sacrifice, The.
Farm-yard Song.
Fortune-Hunter, The.
Goin' Home To-day.
Harry and I.
In the Bottom Drawer.
Last Ride, The.
Learned Negro, The.
Little Puzzler, The.
Man with a Cold in his Head, The.
Merchant of Venice, Trial Scene.
Modest Cousin, The.
Militia General, A.
"Nearer, my God, to Thee."

Old Ways and the New, The.
Opening of the Piano, The.
Our Visitor, and What He came for.
Over the River.
Paddock Elms, The.
Pickwickians on Ice, The.
Picture, A.
Press On.
Possession.
Quaker Meeting, The.
Queen Mab.
Rescue, The.
Shadow on the Wall, The.
Short Sermon, A.
Sisters, The.
Sunday Morning.
There is no Death.
Tobe's Monument.
Toothache.
Tragical Tale of the Tropics, A.
Traveller's Evening Song, A.
Two Anchors, The.
Two Irish Idyls.
What's the Matter with that Nose?
Workers and Thinkers.

Contents of Reading-Club No. 3.

Appeal in Behalf of American Liberty.
Ambition.
Auction Mad.
Aurelia's Unfortunate Young Man.
Ballad of the Oysterman, The.
Bob Cratchit's Christmas-Dinner.
Bone and Sinew and Brain.
Bunker Hill.
Burial of the Dane, The.
Church of the Best Licks, The.
Countess and the Serf, The.
Deck-Hand and the Mule, The.
Evils of Ignorance, The.
First Snow-fall, The.
Flower-mission, Junior, The.
For Love.
Fra Giacomo.
How Persimmons took Cah ob der Baby.
Jonesville Singin' Quire, The.
Last Tilt, The.
Lay of Real Life, A.
Law of Kindness, The.
Losses.
Mad Luce.
Minute-men of '75, The.

Mosquitoes.
Mr. Stiver's Horse.
Ode.
Old Fogy Man, The.
Pat and the Oysters.
Recantation of Galileo, The.
Roast Pig. A Bit of Lamb.
Roman Soldier, The.
Riding down.
Schneider's Tomatoes.
School of Reform, Scenes from the.
Similia Similibus.
Singer, The.
Solemn Book-Agent, The.
Sons of New England, The.
Speech of the Hon. Perverse Peabody on the Acquisition of Cuba.
Temperance.
Twilight.
Two Loves and a Life.
Two Births.
Uncle Reuben's Baptism,
Victories of Peace, The.
Wedding-Fee, The.
Wolves, The.
What the Old Man said.

Contents of Reading-Club No. 4.

Battle Flag of Sigurd, The.
"Business" in Mississippi.
Bell of Atri, The.
Cane-bottomed Chair, The.
Cobbler's Secret, The.
Cuddle Doon.
Custer's Last Charge.
Daddy Worthless.
Decoration.
Dignity of Labor, The.
Elder Sniffle's Courtship.
Goin' Somewhere.
Grandfather.
He Giveth His Beloved Sleep.
Hot Roasted Chestnut, The.
House-top Saint, The.
"Hunchback," Scene from the.
Indian's Claim, The.
Joan of Arc.
Leedle Yawcob Strauss.
Little Black-eyed Rebel, The.
Little Hero, The.
Little Shoe, A.
Lost Cats, The.
Mary Maloney's Philosophy.

Minot's Ledge.
Mother's Fool.
Mr. O'Hoolahan's Mistake.
Mr. Watkins celebrates.
My Neighbor's Baby.
Palmetto and the Pine, The.
Pip's Fight.
Post-Boy, The.
Pride of Battery B, The.
"Palace o' the King, The."
Paper don't Say, The.
Penny ye meant to gi'e, The.
Question, A.
Robert of Lincoln.
Song of the Dying, The.
St. John the Aged.
Tramp, The.
Tom.
Two Portraits.
Village Sewing Society, The.
Way Astors are Made, The.
What is a Minority?
Widder Green's Last Words.
William Tell.
Zenobia's Defence.

CONTENTS OF READING-CLUB NO. 5.

A Blessing on the Dance.
A Charge with Prince Rupert.
A Mysterious Disappearance.
Art-Matters in Indiana.
A Rhine Legend.
A Watch that "Wanted Cleaning."
An Exciting Contest.
An Indignation-Meeting.
An Irish Wake.
Ballad of a Baker.
Ballad of Constance.
Ballad of Ronald Clare.
Between the Lines.
Burdock's Goat.
Butterwick's Weakness.
Dot Baby off Mine.
Edith helps Things along.
Failed.
Faithful Little Peter.
Five.
From the Sublime to the Ridiculous.
Good-By.
"If We Knew."
Last Redoubt.
Mollie, or Sadie?

Noble Revenge.
Not Dead, but Risen.
"One of the Boys."
Scene from "London Assurance."
Scene from "The Marble Heart."
Sideways.
Somebody's Mother.
Something Spilt.
Tact and Talent.
The Amateur Spelling-Match.
The Blue and Gray.
The Bridge.
The Canteen.
The Dead Doll.
The Flood and the Ark.
The Honest Deacon.
The Kaiser's Feast.
The Little Shoes did it.
The Scotchman at the Play.
The Seven Ages.
The Two Glasses.
Tired Mothers.
Uncle Remus's Revival Hymn.
Whistling in Heaven.
Why Biddy and Pat got Married.

CONTENTS OF READING-CLUB NO. 6.

A Disturbance in Church.
A Disturbed Parent.
A Christmas Carol.
A Miracle.
"A Sweeter Revenge."
An Irish Love-Letter.
Behind Time.
Blind Ned.
Cavalry Charge, The.
Clerical Wit.
"Conquered at Last."
Count Eberhard's Last Foray.
Deaf and Dumb.
Der Shoemaker's Poy.
Down with the Heathen Chinee!
Fight at Lookout.
Fireman's Prayer.
Greeley's Ride.
Great Future.
Immortality.
Joe's Bespeak.
John Chinaman's Protest.
Jim Lane's Last Message.
Mr. Coville proves Mathematics.
Nationality.

One Touch of Nature.
Paddy O'Rafther.
Putty and Varnish.
Reserved Power.
Ship-Boy's Letter.
Sweet Singer of Michigan.
Tacking Ship off Shore.
Tammy's Prize.
Talk about Shooting.
Ten Years after.
The Benediction.
The Changed Cross.
The Fan Drill.
The Farmer's Story.
The Fountain of Youth.
The King's Kiss.
The Palmer's Vision.
The Sergeant of the Fiftieth.
The Well-Digger.
"Them Yankee Blankits."
They Met.
Virginius to the Roman Army.
Warning to Woman.
Weaving the Web.
Widow Stebbins on Homœopathy.

CONTENTS OF READING-CLUB NO. 7.

A College Widow.
A Free Seat.
A Humorous Dare-Devil.
All's Well that ends Well.
A London Bee Story.
A Modern Heroine.
A Modern Sermon.
A Reminiscence.
A Royal Princess.
Ave Maria.
Civil War.
Creeds of the Bells.
"Dashing Rod," Trooper.
Down Hill with the Brakes off.
Drawing Water.
Family Portraits.
Fool's Prayer.
Greatest Walk on Record.
Hannibal at the Altar.
"He giveth His Beloved Sleep."
Hohenlinden.
How Neighbor Wilkins got Religion.
How Randa went over the River.
Irish Boy and Priest.
Jimmy Butler and the Owl.
Jim Wolfe and the Cats.

Last Hymn.
Left Alone at Eighty.
Maud's Misery.
National Game.
New Dixie.
On the Channel-Boat.
Orient Yourself.
Paddle Your Own Canoe.
Patriot Spy.
Pledge to the Dead.
Pomological Society.
Rhymes at Random.
San Benito.
St. Leo's Toast.
That Cat.
The Carpenter's Wooing, and the
    Sequel.
The Dead Student.
The Ladies.
The Pin.
The Retort.
The Singer' Alms.
This Side and That.
Two Fishers.
Uncle Mellick dines with his Master.

CONTENTS OF READING-CLUB No 8.

A Brick.
A Colored Debating Society.
Along the Line.
A New Version of the Parable of the
    Virgins.
An Evangel.
Annie's Ticket.
Apples — A Comedy.
A Sermon for the Sisters.
A Thirsty Boy.
Aunt Phillis's Guest.
Ballad of the Bell-Tower.
"Christianos ad Leones!"
City Man and Setting Hen.
Daisy's Faith.
De 'Sperience ob Reb'rend Quacko
    Strong.
Defence of Lucknow.
Dutch Security.
Fast Mail.
Father William.
From One Standpoint.
Girl of the Crisis.
Grave of the Greyhound.
Indian Warrior's Defence.
Labor is Worship.

Lanty Leary.
Last of the Sarpints.
Legend of the White Hand.
London Zoölogical Gardens.
Masked Batteries.
Miss Edith's Modest Request.
Mrs. Brown at the Play.
Old Grimes.
People will laugh.
Peril of the Mines.
Parody on "Father William."
Patter of the Shingle.
Paul Clifford's Defence.
Shiftless Neighbor Ball.
Song of the Mystic.
The Baron's Last Banquet.
The Captive.
The Dilemma.
The Divorce Feast.
The Farmer and the Barrister.
The Man with a Bear.
The Story of the Tiles.
The Outlaw's Yarn.
The Rich Man and the Poor Man.
Two Dreams.
Yankee Courtship.

CONTENTS OF READING-CLUB NO. 9.

Antoinette.
Antony to Cleopatra.
Awfully Lovely Philosophy.
Calif, The.
Cheek.
Claribel's Prayer.
Cleopatra Dying.
Dagger Scene from "The Wife," The.
Dandy Fifth, The.
Don Squixet's Ghost.
Gingerbread.
Hannah.
"He and She."
Hero Woman, The.
Holly Branch, The.
Jan Steener's Ride.
Johnny on Snakes.
King's Bell, The.
Legend of Saint Barbara, The.
Legend of the Organ-Builder.
Life in Death.
Little Girl's Song, The.
Lookout Mountain.
Loves of Lucinda.
Man Wich didn't drink Wotter, The.

Make the Best of Every Thing.
Marked Grave, The.
Marriage of Santa Claus, The.
Mice at Play.
No Color Line in Heaven.
Night Watch.
Old Man's Dreams, An.
One-legged Goose, The.
Owl Critic, The.
"Papa says so too."
Poetry of Iron, The.
Right must win, The.
Reviving de Sinners.
Selling the Farm.
Setting a Hen.
She would be a Mason.
Similar Case, A.
Sleep, The.
Song of the North, The.
Spinning-wheel, The.
Time.
Tomato, The.
Tramp of Shiloh, The.
Very Naughty Little Girl's Views.
Widow of Nain, The.

CONTENTS OF READING-CLUB NO. 10.

Autumn Leaves.
Autumn Thoughts.
Baffled Book-Agent, The.
Banker and the Cobbler, The.
Brudder Johnson on 'Lectricity.
Building and Being.
Carcassonne.
Chain of Gold, The.
Charge of the Heavy Brigade.
Christmas Elegy, A.
Clown's Baby, The.
Confession, The.
Conversion of Col. Quagg.
Court Lady, A.
Cruise of the "Monitor," The.
Death of the Old Wife.
Death of Steerforth.
Garfield.
Hark!
How the Colonel took It.
Intensely Utter.
Jackdaw of Rheims, The.
Mate of the "Betsy Jane," The.
Nebuchadnezzah.
No Time like the Old Time.

No Yearning for the Beautiful.
"Ole Marster's" Christmas.
Our Baby.
Parting Lovers, The.
Penitent, A.
Purpose, A.
Round of Life, The.
Ramon.
Rather Embarrassing.
Ravenswood's Oath.
Robert Emmett's Last Speech.
Saving Mother.
Scene from "Mary Stuart."
Serenade, The.
Sharpshooter's Miss, The.
Sooner or Later.
Story of a Stowaway, The.
Squire Houston's Marriage Ceremony.
The Way Rube Hoffenstein sells.
This means You, Girls.
Tickled All Oafer.
Union of Blue and Gray.
Widow to Her Son, The.
Wild Weather Outside.
Young Grimes.

CONTENTS OF READING-CLUB NO. 11.

Abraham Lincoln and the Poor Woman.
Big Ben Bolton.
Bivouac of the Dead, The.
Captain's Tale, The.
Cataract of Lodore, The.
Charge at Valley Maloy, The.
Child's Evening Prayer, The.
Clear Bargain, A.
Closing Scene, The.
Convent Robbing.
Countersign was "Mary," The.
Crutch in the Corner.
Drifted Out to Sea.
"Fall In."
For Life and Death.
Glimpse of Death, A.
Going towards Sundown.
Garibaldi and His Companions.
Kelly's Ferry.
Last upon the Roll.
Leedle Yawcob Strauss: What He says.
Magnificent Poverty.
Mr. Murphy explains His Son's Conduct.
Mysterious Rappings.

Nearer Home.
No Precedent.
Old Man goes to Town, The.
O'thello.
"Mebbe," Joe's True Feesh Story.
Paddy's Metamorphosis.
Pat's Bondsman.
Pericles to the People.
"Picciola."
Red O'Neil, The.
Reflections on the Needle.
Roland Gray.
Second Review of the Grand Army.
Silver Cup, The.
Snow-storm, The.
Speculation.
Suckers on de Corn.
"Treadwater Jim."
Unforgotten Foe, The.
Variegated Dogs.
Virginny.
Washee, Washee.
What saved the Union.
Wonderful Tar Baby Story, The.
Wreck of the White Ship.
Yawcob Strauss.

CONTENTS OF READING-CLUB NO. 12.

Æsthetic Housekeeper, The.
Asking the Gov'nor.
Asleep at the Switch.
Awkward.
Bad Mix, A.
Boys Who Never got Home, The.
Concurrent Testimony.
Cruise of the "Nancy Jane," The.
Discontented Pendulum, The.
Doctor's Wedding, The.
Enoch of Calaveras, The.
Fire! Fire!
Fire-Worshippers, The.
Funny Small Boy, The.
Good-by, Proud World.
How Dennis took the Pledge.
How He Made It.
How Tim's Prayer was answered.
House that Jack built, The.
Ideal of Woman, An.
I have drank my Last Glass, Boys.
Jack at All Trades, A.
Judge Pitman's Watch.
Katie's Answer.
Little Presbyterian Maid, The.
Little Rocket's Christmas.

Lucille's Mistake.
Making Love in the Choir.
Memory.
Money Musk.
Mike McGaffaty's Dog.
Nancy Sykes.
New Church Doctrine, The.
Night after Christmas, The.
"Norval."
Old Knight's Treasure, The.
Only a Crippled Soldier.
Pat and the Pig.
Pegging Away.
Penn's Monument.
Policeman's Story, The.
Postilion of Nagold, The.
Public Grindstone, The.
Scene from "Leah the Forsaken."
Soldiers' Monument, The.
Signing the Pledge.
Sun-Burst.
The Three Little Chairs.
Two Ways of Telling a Story.
Veterans, The.
War with Alcohol, The.

CONTENTS OF READING-CLUB NO. 13.

Apele for Are to the Sextant, A.
Art is Pitiless.
"Assorted" Declamation, An.
Auction Extraordinary.
Bob.
Candor.
Chicken Talk.
Choosing a Cow.
Christmas Ballad, A.
Cold Water.
Colored Sermon, A.
Death of Mogg Megone, The.
Death of the Dominie, The.
Death of Thomas Becket, The.
Drinking a Tear.
Eaglet and the Child, The.
Goin' to Liza's.
Gridiron, The.
How Vera Cruz was won.
"Jesus, Lover of My Soul."
Lady Yeardley's Guest.
Little Elfin's Plea.
"Little Potter's" Story.
"Make It Four, Yer Honor."
Middlerib's Rheumatic Cure.

Mount of the Holy Cross, The.
Mr. Collins's Croquet-Set.
Old Maid's Prayer, The.
Old Twine String, The.
"O'Meara Consolidated," The.
Orphan Boy, The.
"Peace, Be Still."
Piece of Bunting, A.
Planchette.
Political Outfit, A.
Popping Corn.
Railroad-Crossing, The.
Ram for Ould Oireland, A.
Ruined Man, The.
Sacred Relics of the Past.
Sequel to the Old Maid's Prayer.
Statue Scene, The.
Story of the Swords, The.
Sunset Prophecy, A.
Ticket o' Leave.
Tipperary.
"Tom's Dead!"
Vengeance, A.
"Willie."
Wisdom of Ali, The.

CONTENTS OF READING-CLUB NO. 14.

Advanced Thought.
African Chief, The.
American Flag, The.
Bad Boy at Breakfast, The.
Ballad of Cassandra Brown, The.
Catastrophe, A.
Caught by the Tide.
Charge by the Ford, The.
Charity : A Problem.
Clouds, The.
Confession, The.
Curfew Heroine, The.
Deacon's Prayer, The.
Dot Delephone.
Drift.
Good Wife, The.
How He Won Her.
In the Floods.
Irish Philosopher, The.
Judge's Search for a Waterfall, The.
King and the Snake, The.
Knife-Grinder, The.
Like Mother used to make.
Little Jesse James.
"Lord's Plate," The.

New-style Poem, A.
Nine Suitors, The.
Not to be Won that Way.
O'Branigan's Drill.
O'Connell as an Orator.
Old Daddy Turner.
Old Puritan Divines, The.
Oratory of Wendell Phillips.
Paddy's Excelsior.
Pat's Dream of Heaven.
Plantation Proverbs.
Prospective.
Regulus to the Roman Senate.
Rolla's Address to the Peruvians.
Roll-Call.
Scene from "Sweethearts."
Scene from "The Iron Chest."
Serious Jar, A.
Sheridan's Ride.
Society Play, A.
Soldier's Reprieve, The.
Somebody's Darling.
Unknown.
Virginia.
Why No Scotchmen go to Heaven.

FOR SCHOOL EXERCISES AND EXHIBITIONS.

PARLOR VARIETIES (Part III.). Plays, Pantomimes, Charades. By OLIVIA LOVELL WILSON. Containing nineteen bright and witty entertainments for amateur actors. Boards, 50 cents; paper, 30 cents.

PARLOR VARIETIES (Part I.). Plays, Pantomimes, and Charades. By EMMA E. BREWSTER. 16mo. Boards, 50 cents; paper, 30 cents.

PARLOR VARIETIES (Part II.). Tableaux, Dialogues, Pantomimes, etc. By EMMA E. BREWSTER and LIZZIE B. SCRIBNER. Boards, 50 cents; paper, 30 cents.

A BAKER'S DOZEN. Humorous Dialogues. Containing thirteen popular pieces. Seven for male characters; six for female characters. Boards, 60 cents.

THE GLOBE DRAMA. A new collection of original Dramas and Comedies. By GEORGE M. BAKER. Author of Amateur Dramas, etc. Illustrated. $1.50.

BALLADS IN BLACK. By F. E. CHASE and J. F. GOODRIDGE. A Series of Original Readings, to be produced as *Shadow Pantomimes.* With full directions for representation, by F. E. CHASE. Illustrated with fifty full-page Silhouettes, by J. F. Goodridge; containing the following Pantomimes: Drink, Driggs and his Drouble, Orpheus the Organ-Grinder, Anonymous, Cinderella, In Pawn. Price in boards, illustrated cover, oblong, $1.00; each ballad separate, in paper, 25 cents.

THE BOOK OF ELOQUENCE. A Collection of Extracts, in Prose and Verse, from the most famous Orators and Poets. New edition. By CHARLES DUDLEY WARNER. Cloth, $1.50.

DIALOGUES FROM DICKENS. For schools and home amusement. Selected and arranged by W. ELIOT FETTE, A.M. First Series, Illustrated. Cloth, $1.00. Second Series, Illustrated. Cloth, $1.00. The Dialogues in the above books are selected from the best points of the stories, and can be extended by taking several scenes together.

SOCIAL CHARADES AND PARLOR OPERA. By M. T. CALDER. Containing Operas, Charades, with Popular Tunes. Boards, 50 cents; paper, 30 cents.

POETICAL DRAMAS. For home and school. By MARY S. COBB. Containing Short Poetical and Sacred Dramas, suitable for Sunday-school entertainments, etc. Boards, 50 cents; paper, 30 cents.

FOOTLIGHT FROLICS. School Opera, Charades, and Plays. By Mrs. CHARLES E. FERNALD. Thirteen entertainments, including "Christmas Capers," a capital "Tree" introduction. Boards, 50 cents; paper, 30 cents.

COBWEBS. A Juvenile Operetta. By Mrs. ELIZABETH P. GOODRICH, author of "Young Folks' Opera," etc. 50 cents.

MOTHER GOOSE MASQUERADES. (The Lawrence Mother Goose.) By E. D. K. Containing full directions for getting up an "Evening of Nonsense," Shadow-Plays, Pantomimes, Processions, Mimic Tableaux, and all the favorite ways of delineating passages of Mother Goose. *Just the book for exhibitions.* 50 cents net.

YOUNG FOLKS' OPERA. An illustrated volume of Original Music and Words, bright, light, and sensible. By that favorite composer for the young, Mrs. ELIZABETH PARSONS GOODRICH. 8vo. Boards. $1.00.

Sold by all booksellers and newsdealers, and sent by mail, postpaid, on receipt of price.

LEE & SHEPARD, Publishers, Boston.

NEW ELOCUTIONARY HAND-BOOKS

EDITED BY GEORGE M. BAKER.

IRISH DIALECT RECITATIONS. A series of the most popular Readings and Recitations in prose and verse. Boards, 50 cents; paper, 30 cents.

NEGRO DIALECT RECITATIONS. A series of the most popular Readings in prose and verse. Boards, 50 cents; paper, 30 cents.

THE GRAND ARMY SPEAKER. A collection of the best Readings and Recitations on the Civil War. Boards, 50 cents; paper, 30 cents.

YANKEE DIALECT RECITATIONS. A humorous collection of the best Stories and Poems for Reading and Recitations. Boards, 50 cents; paper, 30 cents.

MEDLEY DIALECT RECITATIONS. A series of the most popular German, French, and Scotch Readings. Boards, 50 cents; paper, 30 cents.

THE READING CLUB and Handy Speaker, No. 18. Paper, 15 cents. Uniform with Nos. 1 to 17.

BAKER'S HUMOROUS SPEAKER. A compilation of popular selections in and verse in Irish, Dutch, Negro, and Yankee dialect. Uniform with "The Handy Spe "The Prize Speaker," "The Popular Speaker," "The Premium Speaker." Cloth, $1.0

Sold by all Booksellers, and sent by mail, postpaid, on receipt of price the publishers, **LEE & SHEPARD, Boston**

www.ingramcontent.com/pod-product-compliance
Lightning Source LLC
Chambersburg PA
CBHW030559270326
41927CB00007B/983